Gold
EXPERIENCE

A1

Pre-Key for Schools

T0351910

Vocabulary
and Grammar
Workbook

Lucy Frino

Contents

Hello!

VOCABULARY

1 **Match 1–7 with a–g to make sentences.**

1 My name's
2 I'm
3 My sister
4 We're from
5 Nice to
6 What's your
7 How old

a eleven.
b are you?
c is fourteen.
d Isabel.
e Spain.
f meet you.
g name?

2 **Find eight family words.**

d	e	b	r	g	o	u	s	m	u	m
a	u	n	w	r	c	o	u	s	n	u
p	i	a	d	a	d	s	a	o	c	t
o	b	v	a	n	t	c	i	g	l	h
g	r	a	n	d	m	o	t	h	e	r
r	o	f	h	f	l	u	w	o	h	i
a	t	g	r	a	w	s	y	d	c	k
c	h	h	z	t	e	i	n	a	v	e
f	e	u	i	h	f	n	o	m	u	p
e	r	c	l	e	l	i	t	o	j	n
r	a	n	d	r	o	a	u	n	t	r

1 _mum_   5 ....
2 ....   6 ....
3 ....   7 ....
4 ....   8 ....

3 **Look at the photos of Mia's family. Complete the sentences with these words.**

aunt   brother   cousin   dad
grandparents   ~~mum~~   uncle

This is me and my 1) _mum_ , Annie. And this is my 2) .... He's 10.
Here's my 3) ...., Ewan. In this photo he's with my 4) ...., Ava and George.
This is my 5) ...., Scott and my 6) ...., Jessica. They're with my 7) ...., Rob. He's five.

4 **Rearrange the letters to make countries.**

1 insap   S_pain_
2 eth sau   t..........
3 anich   C..........
4 tkyure   T..........
5 dplano   P..........
6 tiiarbn   B..........
7 saliautra   A..........

5 **Complete the table with these words.**

~~bag~~   basketball   cat   football   mouse
picture   ruler   swimming

objects	sports	animals
1) _bag_	4)	7) ....
2)	5)	8) ....
3)	6)	

GRAMMAR

1 Choose the correct answer, A, B or C.

1 This _____is_____ my cousin. He's eighteen.
   A are   **B** is   **C** be

2 My sisters _____ ten and nineteen.
   A are   **B** is   **C** be

3 Rafal _____ from Poland.
   A 'm   **B** 're   **C** 's

4 That _____ my dog.
   A aren't   **B** isn't   **C** am not

5 Joshua and Lily _____ from Britain.
   A aren't   **B** isn't   **C** is not

6 Here _____ our cats, Michel and Martha.
   A is   **B** are   **C** this

7 I _____ from Mexico.
   A 's   **B** 're   **C** 'm

2 Put the words in the correct order to make questions.

1 name? / 's / your / What
   What's your name?

2 you? / are / old / How

3 colour? / favourite / your / What / 's

4 favourite / 's / singer? / your / Who

5 your / What / TV / favourite / 's / channel?

6 Is / this / sister's / your / bag?

3 Make positive (+) or negative (–) short answers.

1 Is Sergio from Malawi? (–)   *No, he isn't.*
2 Is Maria from Turkey? (–)
3 Is Paul from the USA? (+)
4 Are you from Britain? (+)
5 Is this Annabelle's book? (+)
6 Is this Celia's pen? (–)
7 Are these Luca's pencils? (+)
8 Are these red pens? (–)

4 Match the pets with the people. Make sentences.

1 Carmen   **2** Tom   **3** Georgina

4 Yuri   **5** Natalie   **6** John

 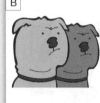 

A *3* *These are Georgina's cats.*
B
C
D
E
F

5 Make sentences. Use *that* or *those*.

1 Elaine / pictures
   Those are Elaine's pictures.

2 Daniel / ruler

3 Amelia / dog

4 my cousin / pens

5 my mum / sister

6 Josef / books

5

01 My space

VOCABULARY

1 Match the picture with these words.

> clock   computer   cupboard   curtains
> ~~desk~~   electric guitar   shelf

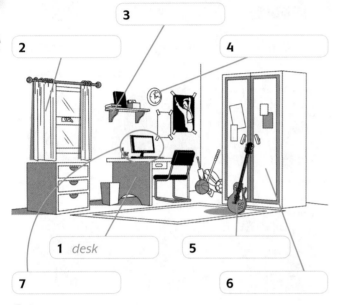

3

2

4

1 *desk*

5

7

6

2 Rearrange the letters to make things in a room.

1	oclkc	*clock*
2	vlesshe	
3	trespo	
4	aiurtcns	
5	iemobl ohpen	
6	scimu yerpal	

3 Complete the table with these words. There are two words you do not need.

> ~~comic~~   cupboard   curtains
> electric guitar   mobile phone
> music player   noticeboard   poster

Read	Listen to
1) *comic*	4)
2)	5)
3)	6)

4 Read the clues. Complete the crossword puzzle.

1 It's above my computer. It's a l _i_ g _h_ _t_ .
2 I read it. It's a c_____ _____c.
3 It's under my desk. It's my b_____n.
4 I sit on it. It's a c_____sh_____ _____ _____.
5 They're next to the window. They're c_____ta_____ns.
6 It's near my desk. I sit on it. It's my ch_____ _____ _____.

```
        ¹
        L
² □ □ □  I □ □
        G        ³
     ⁴           □
     □ □ H □
⁵ □  T □ □ □ □
  □              
  □              
⁶ □ □ □ □        
  □              
  □              
  □              
```

5 Look at the pictures. Complete the sentences.

1   2

3   4

1 The comic is _____*in*_____ the bin.
2 The mouse is _____ the cupboard.
3 The mobile phone is _____ the desk.
4 The clock is _____ the shelf.

6 Choose the correct words.

1 kitchen / bathroom / __garage__
2 bathroom / bedroom / balcony
3 garden / lift / balcony
4 living room / dining room / bedroom
5 lift / balcony / living room
6 bathroom / stairs / kitchen

7 Match the picture with these words.

~~bathroom~~   bedroom   downstairs
kitchen   living room   stairs   upstairs

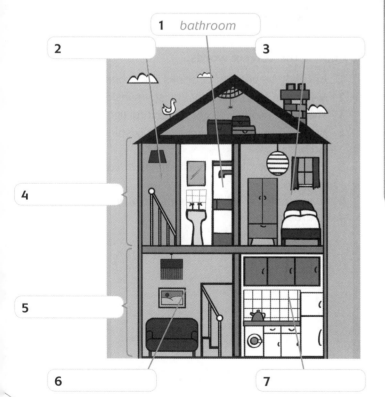

1 _bathroom_
2
3
4
5
6
7

8 Choose the correct answer, A, B or C.

1 I like cooking. Yum! The ___kitchen___ is my favourite room.
   A bathroom   **(B)** kitchen   **C** balcony
2 There's a _____ next to my house. My mum and dad's car is there.
   A balcony   **B** lift   **C** garage
3 I'm from Spain. There's a _____ outside my flat.
   A balcony   **B** bedroom   **C** stairs
4 I'm from Australia. There's a swimming pool in my _____.
   A bedroom   **B** garden   **C** kitchen
5 There are two _____ in my house – one for my mum and dad, and one for me and my brothers and sisters.
   A stairs   **B** bathrooms   **C** downstairs
6 We like parties. There is a big _____ in our house, with a table and ten chairs.
   A dining room   **B** bathroom   **C** garage

9 Complete the text with these words.

bedrooms   garage   garden   lift
living room   ~~swimming pool~~

Hi, welcome to my house! There's a very big 1) _swimming pool_ in the 2) _____. Swimming is cool. Downstairs is my favourite room – the 3) _____. My piano and my guitar are there. There aren't any stairs in my house – there's a special 4) _____. There are ten 5) _____ upstairs, yes, ten! They're for all my friends. There's a 6) _____ under the house, with six cars inside. Isn't it fantastic?

GRAMMAR
There is/There are

1 Match 1–6 with a–f to make sentences about Mirek's bedroom.

1 There's a — a electric guitar.
2 There are some books b on the shelf.
3 There aren't any c cupboard.
4 There's a d clock on the desk.
5 There isn't an e curtains.
6 There isn't anything in the f desk next to the bed.

2 Look at the room. Answer the questions. Use *Yes, there is/Yes, there are*, or *No, there isn't/No, there aren't*.

1 Is there a bin?   *No, there isn't.*
2 Are there any cushions?
3 Is there a shelf?
4 Are there any lights?
5 Is there a noticeboard?
6 Is there a cupboard?

3 Complete the text with these words.

> a   any   are   aren't   's ×2   some

Hi, I'm Hilaria. There' 1) _____'s_____ my school bag, near the door. What's in my bag? There 2) _____ some trainers and there's 3) _____ football. I love football. There aren't 4) _____ pencils but there are 5) _____ pens. There 6) _____ a notebook for my English homework. There's my mobile phone. There 7) _____ any pictures on it at the moment.

4 Make questions. Use *Is there* or *Are there*.

1 pictures / bedroom
   Are there any pictures in your bedroom?
2 pencil case / bag

3 books / shelves

4 poster / bedroom

5 mobile phone / bag

6 trainers / cupboard

have got

5 Choose the correct words.

1 Angela_'s_/*'ve* got lots of books in her bedroom.
2 My house *has/hasn't* got any stairs inside.
3 The living room*'s/'ve* got a beautiful light.
4 My two pet dogs *has/have* got a cushion in the kitchen.
5 The windows in the bedroom *has/have* got green curtains.
6 Juan Manuel*'s/'ve* got a big music player in his bedroom.

6 Complete the interview with one word in each space. Use contractions.

Man: Good morning, Eve. You 1) ___'ve___ got a fantastic house.

Eve: Thank you. It's an old windmill.

Man: How many rooms 2) _____ it got?

Eve: It 3) _____ got seven rooms. One of the bedrooms is downstairs and it's 4) _____ a living room upstairs.

Man: And how many stairs 5) _____ your house got?

Eve: I don't know! I think 6) _____ 's got 50.

Man: Have 7) _____ got a big bedroom?

Eve: No, I 8) _____. My bedroom is round and it's got small windows, but I love it!

7 Read the answers. Make questions.

1 your / a / flat / Has / got / balcony?
Yes, it has.
_____*Has your flat got a balcony?*_____

2 your / garden? / house / got / Has / a
No, it hasn't.
_____

3 Have / house? / got / stairs / you / your / in
Yes, we have. There are 14 stairs.
_____

4 pets? / got / you / Have
No, I haven't. I don't like animals.
_____

5 apartment / your / lift? / Has / got / a
Yes, it has.
_____

6 Have / a / garage / you / your / outside / house? / got
No, we haven't. We haven't got a car.
_____

8 Choose the correct answer, A, B or C.

1 Has your bedroom got yellow walls?
A Yes, I have.
(B) Yes, it has.
C Yes, we have.

2 Has the flat got a lift?
A No, it hasn't.
B No, I haven't.
C Yes, it is.

3 Have your grandparents got a garden?
A No, they aren't.
B Yes, it is.
C Yes, they have.

4 Have you got a shower in your bathroom?
A Yes, we have.
B No, it isn't.
C No, you haven't.

5 Has Mariano got a desk in his bedroom?
A No, I haven't.
B Yes, he has.
C Yes, there is.

6 Has the cupboard got shelves inside?
A Yes, there are.
B Yes, it has.
C Yes, they have.

9 Make positive (+) or negative (−) short answers.

1 Has your house got a garden? (+)
_____*Yes, it has.*_____

2 Have you got a dining room? (+)
_____

3 Have you got a swimming pool? (−)
_____

4 Has your house got a big kitchen? (+)
_____

5 Has your house got stairs? (−)
_____

6 Have you got three bedrooms in your house? (−)
_____

7 Has your bathroom got a shower? (+)
_____

02 My week

VOCABULARY

1 Complete the diary with the days of the week in the correct order.

Friday ~~Monday~~ Saturday Sunday
Thursday Tuesday Wednesday

Monday

2 Match 1–8 with a–h to make phrases about your day.

1	go to	a	homework
2	have a	b	the shops
3	do my	c	shower
4	get	d	my friends
5	meet	e	TV
6	play	f	to my friends
7	watch	g	computer games
8	talk	h	up

3 Look at the pictures. Complete the sentences.

I I ____do____ ____my____ ___homework___ in the afternoon.
2 I _____ my _____ on Tuesday.
3 I _____ in the evening.
4 I _____ my grandmother on Thursday.
5 I _____ on Saturday.
6 I _____ with my family on Sunday.

4 Put the words in the correct order.

1 in / dressed / morning. / I / get / the
    I get dressed in the morning.
2 have / in / shower / the / I / / a / morning.

3 breakfast / with / my / parents. / have / I

4 I / evening. / watch / in / the / TV

5 to / shops / Wednesday. / I / the / go / on

6 lunch / have / afternoon. / the / I / in

7 meet / friends / Saturday. / I / my / on

5 Choose the correct phrase.

1 have singing lessons/<u>have swimming lessons</u>

2 play volleyball/play computer games

3 play computer games/play the guitar

4 play card games/play football

6 Complete the table with these phrases.

> a party   football   fun   singing lessons
> the drums   ~~to the beach~~   to the cinema
> volleyball

go	have	play
1) _to the beach_	3) _____	6) _____
2) _____	4) _____	7) _____
	5) _____	8) _____

7 Find eight months of the year.

d	j	a	n	u	a	r	y	a
e	w	u	o	s	j	s	c	o
c	t	s	v	d	u	y	e	c
e	o	a	e	i	l	h	o	t
m	r	p	m	u	y	e	l	o
b	e	r	b	o	c	a	g	b
e	n	i	e	a	m	a	y	e
r	p	l	r	s	y	i	b	r
a	a	u	g	u	s	t	e	d

1 _January_   **5** _____
2 _____   **6** _____
3 _____   **7** _____
4 _____   **8** _____

8 Rearrange the letters to make months.

1 rbootce   _October_
2 cramh   _____
3 cebdmere   _____
4 raubefry   _____
5 neuj   _____
6 petmesber   _____

9 Match the pictures with the subjects.

1 _history_   **2** _____

3 _____   **4** _____

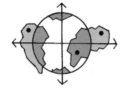 

5 _____   **6** _____

10 Choose the correct words.

1 I have swimming lessons <u>in</u>/on/at June.
2 I do my homework in/on/at Saturday.
3 I watch TV in/on/at 6.00.
4 We go to the cinema in/on/at 8.00.
5 We play volleyball in/on/at July.
6 I meet my friends in/on/at Friday.

11 Complete the sentences with *in*, *on* or *at*.

1 I get up _at_ 8.00.
2 It is the start of the week _____ Monday.
3 We have singing lessons _____ April.
4 Ellen goes to the beach _____ August.
5 I have English class _____ 10.00.
6 My cousins play football _____ Saturday.
7 Karl has lunch _____ 1.00.

GRAMMAR
Present simple

1 **Choose the correct words.**

Life at St Edmund's Music School

School subjects
The school is a music school but the students
1) *has/have* other subjects too, for example, art,
geography and science.

The school day
Students at the school 2) *gets up/get up* at 6.30 in the
morning. They 3) *has/have* lunch at 12.30. The school
day 4) *end/ends* at 7.00 in the evening.

The school week
Students 5) *doesn't/don't* have music classes on
Saturday. The school 6) *don't/doesn't* open on Sunday.

2 **Clara is a student at the music school. Complete what she says with these words.**

> don't ×2   get   have ×3   play   ~~start~~

" I 1) ___*start*___ the day at 6.30. First I
2) _____ dressed and I 3) _____
breakfast. I 4) _____ watch TV in the morning,
there are music lessons! I 5) _____ the piano
in music class and then 6) _____ lunch at
12.00. I 7) _____ play music all day – in the
afternoon we 8) _____ other subjects. I do
my homework in the evening and the day ends at
9.30 at night. "

3 **Choose the correct answer, A or B.**

1 Students at the school ___*play*___ the guitar in
  music classes.
  (A) play   **B** plays
2 They _____ dressed in the morning.
  A get   **B** gets
3 The students _____ computer games at
  school.
  A doesn't play   **B** don't play
4 Ethan _____ breakfast at 7.00 in the
  morning.
  A has   **B** have
5 They _____ science in the afternoons.
  A has   **B** have
6 My sister _____ TV in the afternoon.
  A doesn't watch   **B** don't watch
7 Susan _____ to her friends in the evening.
  A talk   **B** talks
8 Stefano _____ to school on Saturday.
  A go   **B** goes

4 **Rewrite the sentences in the negative form.**

1 Sam gets up at 6.00 in the morning.
  Sam doesn't get up at 6.00 in the morning.
2 His school day starts at 7.00.
  _____
3 Sam's mum and dad watch TV in the afternoon.
  _____
4 Sam's grandmother goes to the shops on Monday.
  _____
5 Sam's sister plays the guitar.
  _____
6 Sam and his sister go to the beach on Sunday.
  _____

5 Choose *do* or *does,* then complete the questions with these verbs.

> end   get up   go   help   ~~like~~   meet   play

1 *Do/<u>Does</u>* your best friend ___*like*___ football?
2 What time *do/does* you _____ in the morning?
3 *Do/Does* your sister _____ volleyball?
4 What time *do/does* your guitar lesson _____ ?
5 *Do/Does* you _____ to English class?
6 *Do/Does* your mother _____ with your homework?
7 What time *do/does* you _____ your friends?

6 Match the questions (1–8) with the answers (a–h).

1 Do you play football?
2 Do your parents go to the cinema?
3 Do you have a brother?
4 Do you have singing lessons?
5 Does your dad play computer games?
6 Do your friends play volleyball?
7 Does your mother go to school?
8 Does your best friend study English?

a No, I don't. I like to play the guitar.
b Yes, they do. They play on Saturday.
c No, she doesn't. She's 42.
d Yes, I do. His name is Pedro.
e Yes, he does. He's in my class.
f No, he doesn't. He watches TV.
g Yes, they do. They like films.
h Yes, I do. I play on Saturday.

7 Choose the correct answer, A, B or C.

1 Does your father have swimming lessons?
   A No, she doesn't.   B No, we don't.
   C No, he doesn't.
2 What time do you have English class?
   A At 10.00.   B Yes, I do.
   C No, they don't.
3 Do you and your friends go to the beach?
   A Yes, they do.   B Yes, I do.
   C Yes, we do.
4 Do your friends have a party every day?
   A No, we don't.   B No, they don't.
   C No, she doesn't.
5 Do you like science?
   A Yes, he does.   B Yes, they do.
   C Yes, I do.
6 Does your sister play the guitar?
   A Yes, she does.   B Yes, he does.
   C Yes, they do.
7 When do you go to bed?
   A In the morning.   B In March.
   C At 9.00 at night.

8 Make questions for a student in Britain.

1 do homework / every day?
   Do you do homework every day?
2 when / get up / in the morning?
   _____
   _____
3 what time / have lunch?
   _____
   _____
4 watch TV / evening?
   _____
   _____
5 go / cinema / weekend?
   _____
   _____
6 play volleyball?
   _____
   _____
7 like / school?
   _____
   _____

Revision Units 1 - 2

VOCABULARY

1 Look at the picture and rearrange the letters to make words.

1	fitl	*lift*
2	brtneiooacd	....
3	uoardpcb	....
4	hirac	....
5	preost	....
6	rissta	....
7	colck	....

2 Choose the correct words.

1 There are <u>curtains</u>/bedrooms next to the window.
2 She plays the guitar/mobile phone.
3 Is your birthday in Friday/February?
4 The books are on/above the shelves.
5 I've got blue cushions/gardens in my bedroom.
6 My house isn't near/next my school.
7 Our computer is downstairs/living room.
8 Your bag is between/on the desk and the chair.

3 Put the months in order.

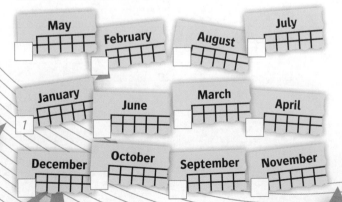

4 Read and choose the best answer, A, B or C.

My 1) ___*cousin*___ Jessica is from the USA. Her mum is my 2) _____'s sister. Saturday for Jessica is different from my Saturday. She 3) _____ up at 8 o'clock and she 4) _____ to the shops. She 5) _____ lunch and then she goes to the 6) _____. In the evening she 7) _____ singing lessons. On Saturday, I 8) _____ football or computer games.

	A		B		C	
1	A uncle		B dad		**C** cousin	
2	A mum		B sister		C grandmother	
3	A goes		B gets		C plays	
4	A gets		B has		C goes	
5	A has		B does		C is	
6	A fun		B dinner		C cinema	
7	A goes		B has		C plays	
8	A play		B go		C get	

5 Look at the timetable. Complete the text with one word in each space.

Monday	Tuesday	
🎨	X + Y / = (triangle)	
🎨	⚗️	
Lunch	Lunch	Lunch
🌐	🦏 🧑‍🚀	🎨
X + Y / = (triangle)	📖✏️	🎨

" Here's my school timetable. On 1) M___*onday*___ morning I have two 2) a_____ lessons. After lunch I have 3) g_____ and 4) m_____. On 5) _____ morning I have maths, then 6) s_____. That's my favourite subject. In the afternoon I have 7) h_____ and 8) E_____. "

GRAMMAR

1 Choose the correct words.

1 There *'s/are* a swimming pool in my grandfather's garden.
2 There *isn't/aren't* a lift.
3 *Is/Are* there any shelves in your bedroom?
4 Yes, there *are/aren't*.
5 Elena *'ve/'s* got four brothers.
6 We *'ve/'s* got a music player in the living room.
7 *Has/Have* you got a pet?
8 No, I *have/haven't*.

2 Make negative sentences.

1 I / play the drums
     I don't play the drums.
2 my dad / play card games

3 there / be / cupboard / living room

4 there / be / pictures / kitchen

5 there / be / garage / downstairs

6 we / have got / dining room / our house

7 Silvia / have got / desk / her bedroom

3 Complete the questions with the correct verbs.

1 _____*Has*_____ he got a TV in his bedroom?
2 _____ you talk to your friends on your mobile phone?
3 _____ there a bin in the living room?
4 _____ Frank have lunch at school?
5 _____ there electric guitars in this shop?
6 _____ you got a cushion, please?
7 _____ your grandparents go to the beach?
8 _____ this garage got a light?

4 Make positive (+) or negative (−) short answers.

1 Do you get dressed in your bedroom? (+)
     Yes, I do.
2 I don't like lifts. Are there any stairs? (+)

3 Does your mum play computer games? (−)

4 Is there a noticeboard at your school? (+)

5 Has your house got stairs? (−)

6 Have your grandparents got a pet? (−)

5 Complete the email with these words.

don't ~~get up~~ go have ×2 on play

Subject: My school day!

Hi Franklin,
How are you? This week's email is about my school day. At seven o'clock I 1) ___*get up*___ and
2) _____ breakfast with my parents.
I 3) _____ to school at eight o'clock.
We 4) _____ English in the mornings
5) _____ Monday and Wednesday. We
6) _____ have swimming lessons at school.
I swim at the weekend with my friends. I like volleyball. I 7) _____ volleyball on Saturday.
What about you?
Bye for now.
Emily

6 Complete what Katarina says with one word in each space.

View previous comments   Cancel   Share   Post

I 1) ___*'m*___ Katarina. I'm
2) _____ Poland. Here's a
photo 3) _____ me. I've got
a pet dog and my brother
4) _____ got a pet cat.
My dog 5) _____ like the
cat! I 6) _____ my friends
on Saturday, and on Sunday I 7) _____
the guitar. I 8) _____ play football. What
about you?

Write a comment   Support

wild animals

VOCABULARY

1 Look at the photos. Complete the crossword puzzle.

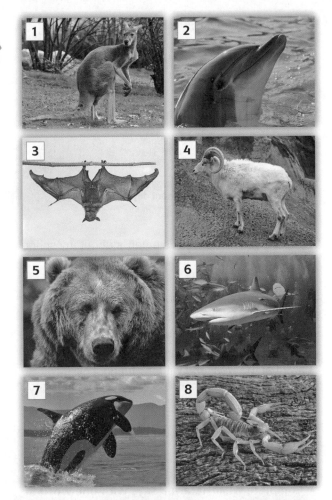

2 Complete the sentences with these animal names.

> bears   ~~camels~~   llamas   meerkats
> pandas   spiders

1 _Camels_ don't drink a lot of water.
2 _____ live in Africa. They've got four legs.
3 _____ are black and white.
4 _____ sleep in the winter.
5 _____ have got eight legs.
6 _____ live in Ecuador. They aren't small.

3 Complete the table with these animals.

> camels   goats   meerkats   ~~scorpions~~
> sharks   whales

They sleep under ground	They work with people	They live in the sea
1) _scorpions_	3) _____	5) _____
2) _____	4) _____	6) _____

4 Put the words about these animals in the correct order.

1 black bear   lives / in / It / the USA.
   It lives in the USA.
2 panda   eats / plants. / It
   _____
3 parrot   has / got / two / legs. / It
   _____
4 snake   It / any / got / hasn't / legs.
   _____
5 meerkat   has / lots / Its / home / got / of / rooms.
   _____
6 scorpion   small / dangerous. / is / It / and
   _____

5 Choose the correct words.

1 Parrots usually live in a *river/jungle*.
2 Fish always live in *water/a cave*.
3 Pandas usually live *in a river/on a mountain*.
4 Camels live in *the sea/a desert*.
5 Bats often live in a *cave/desert*.
6 Spiders sometimes live in *the sea/a forest*.
7 Sharks never live in *lakes/the sea*.
8 Kangaroos always live *in rivers/on land*.

6 Complete the words. Use the photos to help you.

1 h *o p*
2 r _____
3 f _____
4 w _____
5 s _____
6 j _____

7 Are the sentences (1–7) true (T) or false (F)?

1 Whales jump.   *F*
2 Sharks swim.   _____
3 Parrots fly.   _____
4 Goats walk.   _____
5 Dolphins hop.   _____
6 Bats run.   _____

8 Choose the best answer, A, B or C.

1 Bears sometimes *swim* in rivers and lakes.
   A fly   B run   (C) swim
2 Snakes don't walk or run, but some snakes _____.
   A swims   B swim   C hop
3 Bats _____ at night to look for food.
   A fly   B jump   C run
4 Meerkats _____ on four legs and sometimes stand on two legs.
   A run   B swim   C hop
5 Goats don't _____.
   A fly   B jump   C walk
6 Dolphins _____ in some rivers in South America.
   A walk   B swim   C fly

9 Make sentences about the animals. Use a verb from Box 1 and a noun from Box 2.

Box 1

~~fly~~   eat   not like   sleep   swim   walk

Box 2

caves   desert   ~~forest~~   sea
spiders   water

1 Parrots
Parrots fly in the forest.
2 Sharks
_____
3 Camels
_____
4 Bats
_____
5 Cats
_____
6 Meerkats
_____

GRAMMAR
Adverbs of frequency

1 Match 1–6 with a–f to make sentences.

1 Pandas   a don't often drink.

2 Dolphins   b never eat birds.

3 Brown bears   c are often very funny.

4 Camels   d sometimes play games in the water.

5 Meerkats   e sometimes talk.

6 Parrots   f usually sleep in the cold months.

2 Read the article. Choose the correct answer, A, B or C.

> **Subject: Wild kangaroos**
>
> Wild kangaroos 1) _____*always*_____ live in Australia. They usually 2) _____ in groups of about ten. A group of kangaroos is called a mob. They aren't 3) _____ brown. Some kangaroos are grey. Kangaroos only eat plants. They 4) _____ eat spiders or beetles. Kangaroos aren't usually dangerous, but they 5) _____ attack people. Cars are dangerous for kangaroos. In Australia, there 6) _____ often 'kangaroo crossing' signs next to the roads.

1 **A** always   **B** never   **C** don't

2 **A** have   **B** live   **C** talk

3 **A** never   **B** always   **C** sometimes

4 **A** never   **B** always   **C** sometimes

5 **A** always   **B** sometimes   **C** often

6 **A** have   **B** do   **C** are

A kangaroo crossing sign

3 Rewrite the sentences. Put the adverb in brackets in the correct place.

1 Giorgio gets up at eight. (always)

   Giorgio always gets up at eight.

2 He doesn't go to the shops. (usually)

3 He meets his friends on Saturday. (sometimes)

4 He's happy. (usually)

5 Giorgio watches TV. (never)

6 He doesn't go to the cinema. (often)

7 He plays football. (often)

8 His brother is with him. (usually)

4 Put the words in the correct order.

1 usually / has / Kasia / her / got / mobile phone.

   Kasia has usually got her mobile phone.

2 She / singing / sometimes / lessons. / has

3 doesn't / play / usually / She / volleyball.

4 drums. / the / never / She / plays

5 often / She / play / games. / computer / doesn't

6 does / usually / her / the / evening. / She / homework / in

Present simple: wh-questions

5 Match the questions (1–6) with the answers (a–f).

1 Where does it live?
2 What does it eat?
3 When does it sleep?
4 Has it got four legs?
5 Does it jump?
6 Is it a goat?

a Yes, it has.
b Yes, it is.
c In the mountains.
d Plants.
e Yes, it does.
f At night.

6 Complete the questions with these words.

~~Do~~ ×2   How   What   When   Where   Why

1 **A** _____Do_____ pandas live in groups?
   B No. They usually live alone.
2 **A** _____ do wild pandas live?
   B In China.
3 **A** _____ do they sleep?
   B At night.
4 **A** _____ do they eat?
   B Bamboo.
5 **A** _____ do they get their food?
   B They find it in the forest.
6 **A** _____ pandas swim?
   B Yes, they do.
7 **A** _____ don't pandas sleep in the cold months?
   B Because they eat every day.

7 Put the words in the correct order to make questions. Then choose the correct answer.

1 do/stand/on/two/legs/Why/meerkats
   Why do meerkats stand on two legs?
   <u>To look for dangerous animals.</u>/To look for food.
2 bats/for/live/Do/30/years?
   ....
   Yes, they do./No, they don't.
3 live?/Where/kangaroos/do
   ....
   In Africa./In Australia.
4 What/do/meerkats/play?/game
   ....
   Volleyball./Hide-and-seek.
5 do/sloths/eat?/When
   ....
   At night./In the morning.
6 lions/food?/their/How/get/do
   ....
   They find plants./They hunt.

8 Read the answers. Make questions.

1 ...._Where are you from?_.............
   I'm from Argentina.
2 ....
   My name's Josefina.
3 ....
   J – O – S – E – F – I – N – A
4 ....
   I live in Buenos Aires.
5 ....
   I'm 13.
6 ....
   My best friend is Pilar.
7 ....
   My favourite sport is basketball.

04 Around town

VOCABULARY

1 Rearrange the letters to make places in town.

1 knba   *bank*
2 usuemm   _____
3 rgdbie   _____
4 glivael   _____
5 hptosali   _____
6 sbu atsiotn   _____
7 wotn tneecr   _____
8 trpsos enertc   _____

2 Complete the table with these words.

> cinema   market   park   ~~shop~~   square
> supermarket   theatre

shop at the...	watch in the...	walk in the...
1) *shop*	4) _____	6) _____
2) _____	5) _____	7) _____
3) _____		

3 Look at the picture. Complete the sentences.

1 The swimming pool is next to the ____*park*____ .
2 The _____ is in front of the supermarket.
3 The supermarket is between the _____ and the hospital.
4 The _____ is next to the hospital.
5 The park is near the _____ .
6 The hospital is between the _____ and the café.

4 Read the clues and complete the words.

1 You jump on a bus here.
   b *u s s t o p*
2 You play volleyball here.
   s _____   c _____
3 It's a big place with shops or a market, but it isn't a city.
   t _____
4 You walk your dog or play football here.
   p _____
5 You watch films here.
   c _____
6 There are many buses here.
   b _____ s _____

5 Read the text and choose the best answer, A, B or C.

Rome is a very interesting 1) ____*city*____ . There are lots of 2) _____ with important pictures. The River Tevere has got 31 3) _____ . Next to the river there are restaurants and 4) _____ . In the evening, buy a ticket and go to the 5) _____ to watch a play, or walk in a beautiful 6) _____ . There are lots of 7) _____ on the streets or you can go by taxi. Why don't you buy a souvenir at one of the many 8) _____ ?

	A	B	C
1	village	square	ⓒ city
2	hospitals	museums	bridges
3	cafés	bridges	theatres
4	cafés	hospitals	sports centres
5	bank	supermarket	theatre
6	hospital	square	bank
7	markets	banks	bus stops
8	shops	parks	bridges

6 Find eight vehicles.

a	s	l	o	r	b	u	p	e
m	e	e	t	i	b	i	k	e
h	l	o	r	r	y	l	u	b
p	i	f	a	n	e	b	o	s
l	o	d	m	o	r	h	i	o
a	t	b	b	e	t	t	v	m
n	j	o	b	u	o	a	k	u
e	r	a	a	g	s	x	o	s
m	o	t	o	r	b	i	k	e

1 *bike*
2
3
4

5
6
7
8

7 Write *air*, *road* or *sea*.

1 car   *road*
2 boat
3 taxi
4 van
5 helicopter
6 bike
7 plane

8 Choose the correct answer, A, B or C.

1 I've got a ____*bike*____ and I always cycle to school.
   A car   **B** bike   **C** lorry

2 I love to fly. I like _____.
   A planes   **B** trams   **C** vans

3 I travel by _____ every day. There's a stop near my house.
   A bike   **B** boat   **C** bus

4 I like to go by _____ on the road. I talk to the driver.
   A helicopter   **B** motorbike   **C** taxi

5 You can travel fast to different cities on a _____. They are fantastic!
   A train   **B** bike   **C** tram

6 My parents take me to my swimming lessons in their _____.
   A plane   **B** car   **C** train

9 Read about Pierre. Choose the best vehicle.

Pierre is from France. He travels in different vehicles. Which vehicle does he use to go …

1 from home to the village shop (500 metres)?
   lorry/bike/boat

2 from home to school (10 kilometres)?
   car/plane/helicopter

3 from home to the town centre (20 kilometres)?
   plane/bus/boat

4 from home to his grandparent's house (100 kilometres)?
   bike/tram/train

5 from the market in the town centre to the cinema (400 metres)
   tram/plane/helicopter

6 from Paris to London (350 kilometres)?
   plane/bike/taxi

10 Complete the text about Lisa's family with these words.

> ~~bike~~   bus   bus station   car   plane   train

"   Every day I ride my 1) ____*bike*____ to the 2) _____. I go by 3) _____ to my school with my friends. My little brother goes by 4) _____ with my mum. My dad goes to work in the city on the 5) _____. He reads a book. My favourite vehicle is a 6) _____. We take one when we go on holiday. "

Lisa

GRAMMAR
Imperatives

1 Match 1–6 with a–f to make imperatives.

1 Wait
2 Sit
3 Don't stand
4 Don't close
5 Please be
6 Don't

a the door!
b here!
c quiet.
d down, please.
e open your books!
f up.

2 Choose the correct place.

1 Don't run. It's dangerous.
   sports centre/swimming pool/park
2 Don't stand up.
   taxi/shop/city
3 Don't take photos.
   museum/village/bridge
4 Please be quiet.
   town centre/cinema/shop
5 Close the doors.
   school/market/bus stop
6 Don't play football.
   park/sports centre/museum
7 Wait here.
   supermarket/café/bus stop

3 Think about each place. Make positive or negative imperatives.

1 cinema (talk)   *Don't talk.*
2 bus (close the doors)   ....
3 museum (touch the pictures)   ....
4 school (listen)   ....
5 hospital (run)   ....
6 town centre (look at the map)   ....

Subject and object pronouns

4 Complete the table.

Subject pronoun	Object pronoun
I	1) .... *me* ....
2)	you
he	3) ....
she	4) ....
5)	it
we	6) ....
7)	them

5 Choose the correct words.

1 We're in the cinema. Don't talk to *I/me*.
2 Look at the pictures in the museum, but don't touch *them/they*.
3 This is the bus stop. Wait here with *we/us*.
4 The theatre is open now. Please get Tom *his/him* ticket.
5 Do you want pictures of the town centre? You can buy *they/them* here.
6 I want a photo of us near the bridge. There's a woman…. ask *she/her*, please!

6 Complete the sentences with the correct pronoun.

1 I'm busy. Don't talk to .... *me* ....
2 Sergio is my best friend. I like .... very much.
3 Don't touch those paintings. .... are very old.
4 The cafe is near the bank. .... is very good.
5 Marta isn't here. Text ....
6 Oh no! Our bus is at the bus stop. Bus! Please wait for ....!
7 There's my aunt. ....'s in front of the supermarket.

Can for ability

7 Look at the table and make sentences. Use *can* or *can't*.

	swim	speak English	play volleyball	run 2km
Stefan	✗	✓	✓	✗
Mireia	✓	✗	✗	✓
Kirsten	✓	✓	✗	✗

1 *Stefan can't swim. He can speak English.*
   He can play volleyball. He can't run 2km.

2 Mireia _____

   _____ .

3 Kirsten _____

   _____ .

8 Match the questions (1–6) with the answers (a–f).

1 Can pandas swim?
2 Can a cat jump?
3 Can you speak English?
4 Can a dog talk?
5 Can your mum play volleyball?
6 Can Prince Charles speak French?

a Yes, I can.
b No, it can't.
c Yes, it can.
d Yes, they can.
e No, she can't.
f Yes, he can.

9 Make short answers for the questions.

1 Can you speak Chinese?   *No, I can't.*
2 Can penguins fly?   _____
3 Can your dad sing?   _____
4 Can your grandmother run fast?   _____
5 Can you and your friends dance?   _____
6 Can your best friend play the drums?   _____
7 Can sharks swim?   _____

Can for permission

10 Make sentences. Use *can* (✓) or *can't* (✗).

1 museum – take photos ✗
   You can't take photos.
2 cinema – talk ✗

3 park – play football ✓

4 swimming pool – run ✗

5 town centre – walk ✓

6 sports centre – play volleyball ✓

7 bank – sing ✗

11 Look at the photos and make questions.

1

go / the theatre
Can I go to the theatre, please?

2

walk / my dog

3

sit / here

4

open / window

5

take / photos

6

jump / in the water

Revision Units 3 – 4

VOCABULARY

1 Look at the photos. Complete the crossword puzzle.

	1	2	3
	S		
	H		
4	O		
	P		
5			
6			
7			

2 Read the clues. Rearrange the letters to make animals and places.

1 They live under the ground in Africa.
rkeetsma _____ *meerkats*____

2 It lives in the desert and it's big.
mecal _____

3 It's usually in the town centre.
uasqre _____

4 It lives in the mountains in Ecuador.
maall _____

5 You usually go here by car to shop.
mpuktserare _____

3 Choose the correct answer, A, B or C.

1 Sit down on the _____*bus*_____ !
  A car   B lorry   Ⓒ bus

2 I cycle to school. My _____ is green and white.
  A tram   B bike   C van

3 Don't _____ in the hospital, please.
  A walk   B run   C go

4 My grandmother often goes to the shops by _____ .
  A taxi   B helicopter   C fly

5 I like to fly to different countries on holiday. I love _____ !
  A bike   B planes   C motorbikes

6 _____ on a bus to go to the town centre.
  A Swim   B Run   C Jump

7 Helicopters usually _____ from city to city.
  A fly   B hop   C walk

4 Complete the postcard with these words.

> boats   café   city   museum   River
> stops   trams   under

Hi Sam,
We're on holiday in Paris! Every morning we have breakfast at a little
1) __*café*__ near our hotel. Then we go by bus around the 2) _____
There are lots of bus 3) _____ .
There aren't any 4) _____ here in Paris (not like Manchester!). In the afternoon we usually visit a
5) _____ .
The 6) _____ Seine is beautiful. There are 7) _____ called bateaux mouches on the river. They go
8) _____ the bridges.
Love,
Emily

GRAMMAR

1 Rewrite the sentences. Put the adverbs in the correct place.

1 Whales are big. (always)
   Whales are always big.

2 I walk to school. (often)

3 Bears swim. (sometimes)

4 Meerkats don't eat at night. (usually)

5 We go to the beach in December. (never)

6 My aunt is in her car. (always)

2 Choose the correct words.

1 *Who/What* do parrots eat?
2 Where *do/does* your dad play volleyball?
3 *When/Where* do scorpions live?
4 How *do/does* you get to the swimming pool?
5 When *do/does* the supermarket open?
6 *What/Why* do you always play computer games?
7 *When/Why* does this bus get to the town centre?

3 Put the words in the correct order.

1 take / photographs / I / can / please?
   Can I take photographs, please?

2 we / have / this afternoon? / party / Can / a

3 can't / on / play / I / football / Friday.

4 watch / please? / we / TV / Can

5 run / this / can't / in / You / museum.

6 can / People / swim / this / in / lake.

7 Felipe / to / run / the / village. / can

4 Look and make sentences.

Don't talk.

5 Complete the conversation with one word in each space.

Boy: Excuse 1) ⎯⎯ *me* ⎯⎯ .
Girl: Yes.
Boy: Are you from this town?
Girl: Yes, I 2) ⎯⎯⎯⎯⎯ .
Boy: 3) ⎯⎯⎯⎯⎯ do I get to the theatre?
Girl: It's here, next to the sports centre. Can
4) ⎯⎯⎯⎯⎯ see?
Boy: Oh, yes. It's not very near. Can I
5) ⎯⎯⎯⎯⎯ by bus?
Girl: Yes, 6) ⎯⎯⎯⎯⎯ can. The number 17. The
bus stop is just there.
Boy: Where 7) ⎯⎯⎯⎯⎯ I buy a ticket?
Girl: You can buy 8) ⎯⎯⎯⎯⎯ on the bus.
Boy: Thanks for your help.
Girl: No problem.

Media magic

VOCABULARY

1 Match the pictures with these jobs.

dancer   film-maker   photographer
police officer   taxi driver   ~~zoo-keeper~~

zoo-keeper

2 What's my job? Read the clues and complete the jobs.

1 I work in the town centre. I sometimes work at night. I'm a p _o_ _l_ _i_ _c_ _e_ o _f_ _f_ _i_ _c_ _e_ _r_.
2 I work in a theatre. I'm an a_____ .
3 I work in a school. I'm a t_____ .
4 I fly helicopters. I'm a p_____ .
5 I play a sport. I'm a b_____ p_____ .
6 I work in a zoo. I'm a z_____ -k_____ .

3 Match the sentences (1–6) with the jobs (a–f).

1 She can act.
2 She can take good photographs.
3 He likes planes.
4 He can dance.
5 She can speak a different language.
6 He likes animals.

a pilot
b dancer
c actor
d photographer
e zoo-keeper
f Spanish teacher

4 Complete the blog about Luisa's family. Use one word in each space.

My family! ⇦ ⇨

Cancel   Share   Post

The people in my family have got lots of different jobs. My dad loves animals but he isn't a zoo-keeper. He takes photographs of people's pets. He's a 1) *photographer* . My mum likes numbers. She's a maths 2) _____ . My brother works at night. He drives a car. He's a taxi 3) _____ . My uncle drives a car too, but it isn't a taxi. He's a police 4) _____ . My aunt loves music. She's a 5) _____ . My grandparents do the same job. My grandfather works in the theatre and my grandmother works in TV. They're 6) _____ , but they're not famous.

Support

5 **Match the symbols with these words.**

cloudy   ~~cold~~   rainy   snowy   sunny   windy

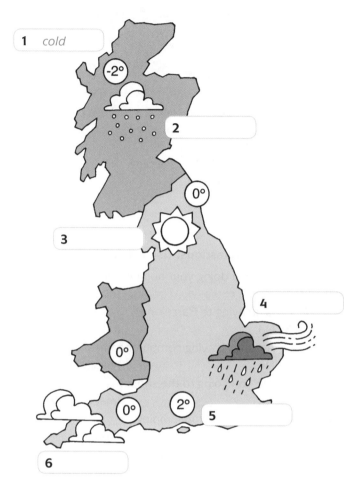

1 cold

2

3

4

5

6

6 **Find six weather words.**

f	w	a	r	m	s	m
o	a	i	a	r	n	s
s	n	o	n	w	o	e
n	c	h	o	d	w	h
o	f	o	g	g	y	o
y	g	t	o	g	a	p
e	w	a	r	l	y	l

1 windy   **4**
2   **5**
3   **6**

7 **Complete the sentences.**

 35°   10°

1 Madrid, Spain   **2** London, England

 22°   -8°

3 Ankara, Turkey   **4** Warsaw, Poland

1 In Madrid it's ___sunny___ and _____ .
2 In London it's _____ and _____ .
3 In Ankara it's _____ and _____ .
4 In Warsaw it's _____ and _____ .

8 **Rearrange the letters to make seasons.**

1 prinsg   ___spring___
2 reumms   _____
3 ntuaum   _____
4 reinwt   _____

9 **Look at the table and complete the sentences.**

Seasons in Britain

March	June	September	December
April	July	October	January
May	August	November	February

1 In Britain, July is in the ___summer___ .
2 September is in the _____ .
3 January is in the _____ .
4 August is in the _____ .
5 March is in the _____ .
6 February is in the _____ .

GRAMMAR
Present continuous: be + verb + -ing

1 Complete the table with the correct present continuous forms.

Positive	I	1) _'m (am)_	
	2) _____	's (is)	having lunch.
	We/You/They	3) _____	
Negative	I	'm (am) not	
	He/She/It	4) _____	5) _____ volleyball.
	6) _____	aren't (are not)	

Don't forget the spelling changes!
get – getting
take – 7) _____

2 Complete the sentences with the verbs in brackets. Use the present continuous.

1 I _'m reading_ (read) a book.
2 My brother _____ (have) breakfast.
3 We _____ (not play) card games.
4 Look! The plane _____ (fly).
5 They _____ (swim) in the sea.
6 I _____ (make) lunch.

3 Put the sentences about Bob's morning in the correct order. Number the lines 1–6.

It's 11 o'clock. Bob and Jock are having a cup of tea. _____
Bob is having a shower. _____
It's seven o'clock. Bob is sleeping. _1_
Bob is getting dressed. _____
Bob is having lunch. _____
Bob is getting up. _____

4 Answer the questions. Use the words in brackets.

1 Q: Are you doing your homework?
   A: No. _I'm playing a game._ (play a game)
2 Q: Is he flying to Barcelona?
   A: No. _____ (take the train)
3 Q: Are they playing computer games?
   A: No. _____ (watch TV)
4 Q: Are you going to the shops?
   A: No. _____ (meet my friends)
5 Q: Is that kangaroo jumping?
   A: No. _____ (hop)
6 Q: Are you playing the piano?
   A: No. _____ (have a singing lesson)

5 Read the email and choose the correct word.

> **Subject: Film-making workshop**
>
> Hi Mum and Dad,
>
> It's day three of my film-making workshop and I 1) *have/'m having* fun! Today I 2) *make/'m making* a film with my friends. I 3) *write/'m writing* this email because our teacher 4) *uses/is using* the camera. She's an actor. She usually 5) *works/'s working* in films and she sometimes 6) *makes/'s making* films, too. I 7) *learn/'m learning* a lot. We 8) *'re having lunch/have lunch* at the moment – the food here is great!
> See you soon.
> Love Sam

Present continuous questions

6 Match the questions (1–6) with the answers (a–f).

1 Is she helping her grandfather?
2 Are you all listening to me?
3 Is he enjoying the party?
4 Are the cats sleeping?
5 Are they acting in your film?
6 Are you talking to your parents, Emmanuel?

a Yes, we are.
b Yes, he is.
c Yes, I am. About the weekend.
d Yes, they are. And they're dancing, too.
e Yes, they are. They're over there.
f Yes, she is.

7 Make positive (+) or negative (–) short answers.

1 Is your brother shouting? (–) _No, he isn't_
2 Amelia, are you having a shower? (–)
   ....
3 Are your parents meeting their friends? (+)
   ....
4 Is she reading a good book? (+) ....
5 Are we watching a film? (+) ....
6 Is the film starting now? (–) ....

8 Make questions.

1 you / enjoy / that book
   Are you enjoying that book?
2 she / have / a guitar lesson
   ....
3 they / get up
   ....
4 he / play / volleyball
   ....
5 they / take / photos
   ....
6 you / film / this
   ....

Present continuous: wh- questions

9 Choose the correct answer, A, B or C.

1 _What_ are you doing?
   A Why   (B) What   C Where
2 .... is the show finishing?
   A What   B Who   C When
3 .... are you taking photos?
   A Why   B Who   C What
4 .... are we having dinner?
   A What   B Who   C Where
5 .... is making breakfast?
   A When   B Who   C Where
6 .... is he watching on TV?
   A What   B Why   C What time

10 Complete the questions with the correct wh-words.

1 _Why_ are you jumping? Are you cold?
2 .... are you learning to dance? Is it in the town centre?
3 .... is filming the show?
4 .... are you having breakfast at 2 o'clock in the afternoon?
5 .... is he checking – the lights?
6 .... is acting at the moment? Is it Sam or Leo?

11 Bartek is at a music festival. Read and complete the telephone conversations. Complete each space with two or three words.

Bartek: Hello?
Henryk: Hi, Bartek. It's Henryk. How are you?
   1) _Are you enjoying_ the music festival?
Bartek: Yes. I'm enjoying it a lot. I love camping, too.
Henryk: 2) .... doing now?
Bartek: I'm walking to the bus stop.
Henryk: 3) .... going to a bus stop?
Bartek: Because the camping isn't next to the arena. Oh … Here's the bus …
Henryk: Bartek?
Bartek: Yes? Is that you, Henryk?
Henryk Yes. Are you at the arena now?
   4) .... watching?
Bartek: I'm watching Frozen Bird. They're really good.
Henryk: Wow! 5) .... they playing?
Bartek: They're playing Walk Away. It's my favourite song! Listen!
Henryk: 6) .... the piano?
Bartek: It's Radek. And Lula's singing.

Fantastic food

VOCABULARY

1 Find eight food words in the word square.

r	c	a	r	r	a	b	r	a	i
m	i	p	s	a	l	e	s	e	d
l	s	c	h	e	e	s	e	g	e
k	c	i	e	e	s	h	g	e	a
m	a	f	o	r	a	n	g	e	l
z	r	u	m	i	l	a	t	r	m
o	r	i	b	e	a	n	s	o	i
i	o	t	y	o	d	u	w	j	l
e	t	o	r	d	e	a	t	s	k

1 _____rice_____   5 _____
2 _____   6 _____
3 _____   7 _____
4 _____   8 _____

2 Complete the food words.

1 s _a_ _l_ _a_ _d_   4 c _____
2 c _____   5 f _____
3 b _____   6 y _____
                     d _____

3 Complete the table with these food words.

~~banana~~ bread chicken egg grapes
milk orange pasta

_____banana_____	_____	_____

4 Choose the correct words.

1 Can I have a chicken _sandwich_/pasta, please?
2 I like cheese/yoghurt drinks.
3 Try some pasta salad/crisps.
4 Do you like banana cheese/milk?
5 Enjoy your orange/chicken salad.
6 I want an vegetable/orange juice, please.

5 Choose the correct answer, A, B or C.

1 Can I have some ___egg___ sandwiches?
   (A) egg   B rice   C milk
2 _____ are good for you.
   A Carrots   B Crisps   C Cheese
3 _____ drinks are my favourite.
   A Pasta   B Bread   C Yoghurt
4 Do you like _____ juice?
   A bean   B rice   C orange
5 I have different types of _____ for my breakfast.
   A pasta   B fruit   C carrot
6 Try some _____ crisps.
   A grape   B milk   C chicken

6 Read the clues, then rearrange the letters to make words about health problems.

1 When you are too hot you have a *temperature* . patteuemrre.

2 Orange juice is good for a _____ . docl

3 I've got a _____ . Keep away! oguch

4 I can't eat carrots. I've got _____ . othchotae

5 Crisps are bad for my _____ . rseo httoar

6 When I eat eggs I get a _____ . omscahtceha

7 Match the words with the photos.

~~cold~~   earache   headache   sore throat
stomachache   toothache

1

cold

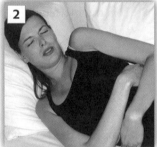

2

3

4

5

6

8 Choose the correct answer, A, B or C.

1 I've got a *temperature* of 39 degrees.
  A cold (B) temperature C cough

2 I can't eat. I've got a _____ .
  A stomachache B earache C cold

3 I can't talk. I've got a _____ .
  A stomachache B sore throat C temperature

4 I'm eating an orange because I've got a
  _____ .
  A toothache B stomachache C cold

5 Be quiet! I've got a _____ .
  A headache B sore throat C cough

6 I can't hear you. I've got _____ .
  A cold B earache C toothache

9 Complete the conversation.

Tara: Hi, Ali. Are you OK?

Ali: No, I feel really 1) h_____*ot*_____ .

Tara: Have you got a 2) t_____ ?

Ali: I don't know. But I've got a 3) s_____
t_____ , too.

Tara: Oh dear. Why don't you go to the doctor's?

Ali: No, I think it's just a 4) c_____ .

10 Read the doctor's advice and make sentences. Use these words and *I've got*.

cold   earache   headache   sore throat
stomachache   ~~temperature~~

1   Stay indoors. Go to bed.

2   Don't listen to your music player.

3   Don't talk too much.

4   Always wash your hands after you clean your nose.

5   Don't eat.

6   Take some medicine. Stay in a quiet place.

1 _____ *I've got a temperature.*
2 _____
3 _____
4 _____
5 _____
6 _____

GRAMMAR
Countable and uncountable nouns (some/any)

1 Complete the table with these food words.

> banana   bread   carrot   chicken sandwich
> fruit   salad   rice   ~~yoghurt drink~~

countable	uncountable
yoghurt drink	

2 Choose the correct answer, A, B or C.

1 I need ___*some*___ bread for my lunch.
   A a   (B) some   C any
2 Are there _____ eggs in the kitchen?
   A an   B any   C a
3 You need to eat _____ orange for your cold.
   A some   B a   C an
4 I want _____ chicken sandwich, please.
   A any   B some   C a
5 There aren't _____ bananas in the fruit salad.
   A any   B an   C a
6 He usually has _____ egg with his rice.
   A some   B an   C any

A lot (of)/much/many

3 Make questions. Use *How much* or *How many*.

1 oranges / you / have got
   How many oranges have you got?
2 rice / be / there
   _____
3 eggs / you / need
   _____
4 carrots / be / there
   _____
5 pasta / you / need
   _____

4 Match the questions (1–6) with the answers (a–f).

1 How many apples are there?
2 Is there much water on the table?
3 How many sandwiches have you got?
4 How much milk have you got?
5 Are there a lot of eggs in the salad?
6 How much rice do you need?

a We haven't got much. Half a litre.
b There are six.
c We need a lot. Two kilos.
d No, there aren't.
e Yes, there's a lot. I'm sorry.
f I haven't got many. Two cheese and one chicken.

5 Complete the sentences with *any*, *some*, *much*, *many* or *a lot*.

1 I don't usually have ___*any*___ coffee with my breakfast. I don't like it.
2 There aren't _____ drinks on the menu, just cola, water and milk.
3 I always have _____ biscuits with hot milk in the morning.
4 How _____ snacks do I eat in a day? _____, I'm sorry to say!
5 My brother doesn't eat _____ fruit. He isn't very healthy.
6 There are _____ of types of pasta.

6 Complete the text with these words.

> a lot of   cheese   egg   ~~fruit~~   not many
> some

School dinners

The food at school is fantastic! In the morning we have a 'snack shop'. There are usually healthy snacks, some 1) ___*fruit*___, like bananas or grapes, and sandwiches. At lunchtime there are hot dinners, but 2) _____ students have the dinners because they have sandwiches from home. There is 3) _____ different food: rice, pasta with tomato sauce, bread, chicken and vegetables. Sometimes I have an 4) _____ with salad and lots of 5) _____. I often have fruit or 6) _____ orange juice. Delicious!

Have to/Don't have to

7 Choose the correct words.

1 I *has to/have to* be at school at eight o'clock.
2 My brother *has to/have to* do a lot of homework.
3 We *has to/have to* wash our hands before we eat.
4 Tomas *has to/have to* eat lots of fruit to be healthy.
5 Students *has to/have to* go home at three o'clock.
6 My sister *has to/have to* practise the guitar a lot.

8 Look at the photos and make sentences.

 1 be quiet
You have to be quiet.

 2 walk
_____

 3 wash hands
_____
_____

 4 be school 8 o'clock
_____
_____

9 Make negative sentences.

1 She has to help at home.
She doesn't have to help at home.
2 I have to do my homework.
_____
3 He has to get up at 7 o'clock at the weekend.
_____
4 We have to play volleyball today.
_____
5 You have to eat salad with pasta.
_____
6 Pasta has to have cheese.
_____

10 Complete the paragraph with the verbs and the correct form of *have to* or *don't have to*.

I play in my school's football team. We
1) *have to practise* (practise) a lot, but we
2) _____ (play) football matches every day.
Sometimes we just run and jump. When there's
a match on a Saturday, I 3) _____ (get up)
early. I go to school by car with my mum to
meet my friends. Then we 4) _____ (go)
to a different town by bus. My mum
5) _____ (watch). She doesn't like football
anyway. When we play we 6) _____ (run)
a lot and we 7) _____ (drink) lots of water.

11 Match the questions (1–7) with the answers (a–g).

1 Do you have to do a lot of homework?
2 Does your dad have to work at night?
3 Do you have to take medicine for a cold?
4 Does your sister have to get up at six o'clock?
5 Do they have to be quiet in the museum?
6 Do I have to go to bed at nine o'clock?
7 Do we have to do the homework for tomorrow?

a No, you don't. You can drink orange juice.
b No, he doesn't.
c Yes, she does.
d Yes, you do.
e Yes, I do. Two hours a day.
f Yes, they do.
g No, we don't. It's for Thursday.

12 Make questions. Use *have to*.

1 you / get up at seven o'clock
Do you have to get up at seven o'clock?
2 your brother / go to the shops today
_____
3 your friends / walk to school
_____
4 your mum / go to work / on Saturday
_____
5 we / meet at the café
_____
6 I / take the dog for a walk
_____

Revision Units 5 – 6

VOCABULARY

1 Choose the correct words.

1 Don't play football today. You've got a _temperature_/toothache and it's cold outside.

2 I sometimes don't work when it's foggy. I'm a _pilot/teacher_.

3 Do you like animals? You can be a _pet/zoo-keeper_.

4 My sister doesn't eat _chicken/juice_.

5 I can't eat that cheese. I've got a _toothache/cold_.

6 I don't want to watch TV. I've got a _stomachache/ headache_.

7 _Carrots/Oranges_ are a type of vegetable.

2 Read the clues and complete the words.

1 I want to be a d _a_ _n_ _c_ _e_ _r_ . I have to practise a lot.

2 James Cameron is a famous film-m _____ _____ _____ from the USA.

3 Juan Carlos Navarro is a basketball p_____ _____ _____ _____ from Spain.

4 I'm a good p_____ _____ _____ _____ _____ _____ _____ . I'm taking photos for a competition.

5 Our teacher can't talk today. She's got a sore t_____ _____ _____ _____ _____ .

6 I've got a headache and a cough. I think I've got a c_____ _____ _____ .

7 Eat some yoghurt. It's good for your s_____ _____ _____ _____ ache.

8 His t_____ _____ _____ _____ _____ _____ _____ is 37 degrees. I think he's OK.

3 Complete the blog with these words.

driver   officer   ~~rainy~~   snowy   spring
warm

My mum works in our town. She has to walk a lot. She often has to work when it's 1) _____rainy_____ , and in the winter, when it's cold and 2) _____ . But she likes her job. She helps people. She's a police 3) _____ . My dad is always in his car. He's a taxi 4) _____ in the city. He likes to work in the 5) _____ , when the weather is 6) _____ , but not too hot.

4 Look at the photos. Complete the crossword puzzle.

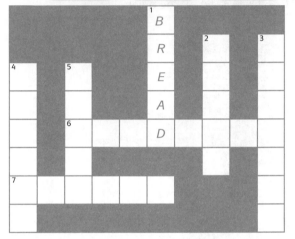

5 Look at the table and complete the sentences.

1 In Buenos Aires in the _summer_ it's hot and sunny.

2 In London in the _____ it's usually windy.

3 The weather in London is often rainy and _____ in the spring.

4 In July in Buenos Aires it's sometimes _____ .

5 _____ in London is from June to August.

6 In January in London it's snowy and _____ .

	Buenos Aires, Argentina	London, England
Spring	September–November 22°	March–May 13°
Summer	December–February 29°	June–August 20°
Autumn	March–May 23°	September–November 10°
Winter	June–August 16°	December–February 7°

GRAMMAR

1 Complete the sentences with the verbs in brackets. Use the present continuous.

1 We __'re writing__ (write) a book about an actor.
2 Be quiet, please! I _____ (do) my homework.
3 Dad _____ (make) breakfast this morning.
4 Justine and Nathalie aren't here. They _____ (play) volleyball.
5 Why are you texting your sister? She _____ (sit) over there!
6 _____ you _____ (go) to the shops?
7 _____ the party _____ (finish) now?
8 _____ the boys _____ (have) a singing lesson at the moment?

2 Put the words in the correct order.

1 playing / drums? / Who / the / is
  Who is playing the drums?
2 they / here? / What / are / doing
  _____
3 on / She's / to / the / talking / phone. / her/ friend
  _____
4 What / watching / now? / you / are
  _____
5 do / You / have / homework. / to / your
  _____
6 have / to / swimming / we / Do / have / lessons?
  _____
7 Pietro / make / Does / have / his / lunch? / to
  _____
8 We / get / up / have / at / to / o'clock. / six
  _____

3 Look at the picture and make sentences. Use There's/There are or There isn't/There aren't.

1 salad   _There's some salad._
2 egg   _____
3 bread   _____
4 oranges   _____
5 bananas   _____
6 crisps   _____
7 pasta   _____

4 Read the conversation. Choose the correct answer, A, B or C.

Maria: We 1) ___'re___ making some sandwiches for the party. How 2) _____ do we have 3) _____ make?

Oscar: About 20.

Maria: That's 4) _____ of sandwiches.

Oscar: I know, but the party is at 12 o'clock. My friends usually 5) _____ a lot at lunchtime.

Maria: OK. Can you get 6) _____ cheese for the sandwiches at the supermarket?

Oscar: Yes. How 7) _____ ?

Maria: 500 grams.

Oscar: Do I have to get 8) _____ drinks?

Maria: No, that's OK. We've got a lot of cola.

1 **(A)** 're	**B** 's	**C** 'm
2 **A** much	**B** many	**C** some
3 **A** we	**B** to	**C** that
4 **A** a lot	**B** many	**C** much
5 **A** 're eating	**B** eats	**C** eat
6 **A** a lot	**B** much	**C** some
7 **A** much	**B** many	**C** do
8 **A** a	**B** any	**C** a lot

5 Complete the sentences with has to or have to in the positive or negative form.

1 Beatríz ___has to___ take some medicine. She's got a temperature.
2 Teachers _____ work at night.
3 Football players _____ run a lot.
4 I _____ go to school in July or August. It's the holidays.
5 My brother _____ do homework. He's only five.
6 She can't sing. She _____ have some lessons!

VOCABULARY

1 Complete the table.

Cardinal number (How many)	Ordinal number (Order)
one	first
1) _____ *two*	second
three	2) _____
four	3) _____
4) _____	fifth
six	5) _____
6) _____	seventh
eight	7) _____
nine	8) _____
ten	tenth

2 Put the dates in the order they happen.

> the twenty-fourth of May
> the twentieth of May   ~~the third of May~~
> the twenty-ninth of May
> the fifteenth of May   the thirty-first of May
> the twelfth of May
> the twenty-fifth of May

1 *the third of May*
2 _____
3 _____
4 _____
5 _____
6 _____
7 _____
8 _____

3 Match the numbers with the way we say the dates.

1 *the first of August*
2 _____
3 _____
4 _____
5 _____
6 _____
7 _____

> the twenty-first of August
> the sixth of August   the sixteenth of August
> ~~the first of August~~   the thirtieth of August
> the thirteenth of August
> the twenty-sixth of August

4 Read and complete the table.

1 In the USA, Independence Day is on the fourth of July.
2 In Poland, Teacher's Day is on the fourteenth of October.
3 In Argentina, the twentieth of June is National Flag Day.
4 In the UK it is Bonfire Night on the fifth of November.
5 The twenty-third of April is special in Turkey. It's Children's Day.
6 Australia Day is on the twenty-sixth of January.

Country	Date	Holiday
USA	4 July	Independence Day
1) _____ *Poland*	2) _____	Teacher's Day
Argentina	3) _____	4) _____
5) _____	5 November	6) _____
Turkey	7) _____	Children's Day
Australia	8) _____	Australia Day

5 Match the way we say the years (1–8) with the numbers (a–h).

1 nineteen twenty   a 2019
2 seventeen hundred   b 2050
3 seventeen fifty-five   c 1902
4 sixteen fifty-five   d 2005
5 twenty nineteen   e 1655
6 nineteen oh two   f 1700
7 two thousand and five   g 1920
8 twenty fifty   h 1755

6 Read the clues. Complete the crossword puzzle.

Down

1 After I play football, I c _*hange*_ my clothes.
2 Do you often t_____ your friends?
5 Does Barbara usually v_____ her grandmother on Saturday?
6 I live near my school, so I w_____ there every morning with my dad.

Across

3 We s_____ with our cousins on holiday.
4 You can t_____ from London to Paris by train, boat or plane.
7 When does the bus a_____ in the town centre?

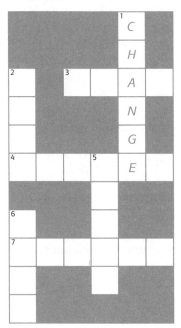

7 Match 1–6 with a–g to make sentences.

1 Ethan travels to his grandfather's house   _*g*_
2 He usually arrives   ....
3 They talk about   ....
4 Ethan helps his granddad in   ....
5 They tidy   ....
6 Then they change   ....
7 After dinner, they walk   ....

a their clothes.
b the garage together.
c in the morning.
d football.
e in the woods with the dog.
f the garden.
g by car.

8 Read and choose the best answer, A, B or C.

Cristina always 1) _*visits*_ her cousins in the spring. They live near the beach. She 2) _____ for a week. She 3) _____ there by car with her mum and dad. They usually 4) _____ in the evening. Cristina and her cousins 5) _____ on the beach every day and they 6) _____ for hours.

1 **A** changes   **B** visits   **C** arrives
2 **A** arrives   **B** tidies   **C** stays
3 **A** talks   **B** walks   **C** travels
4 **A** arrive   **B** stay   **C** change
5 **A** wash   **B** walk   **C** tidy
6 **A** talk   **B** arrive   **C** help

9 Complete the blog with these verbs.

arrive   help   stay   text   walk   ~~wash~~

My family!   ⇦ ⇨

Cancel   Share   Post

Saturday is my favourite day of the week. I usually get up at seven o'clock and I 1) _*wash*_ my hair. I have breakfast and then I 2) _____ my dad at the market. We 3) _____ there because it's near my house. We 4) _____ at about half past eight and we 5) _____ all morning. After lunch I 6) _____ my friends and we go to the cinema or the sports centre. We have lots of fun.

GRAMMAR
Past simple: *be*

1 Choose the correct words.

1 There *was/were* one room in a Frontier House.
2 In 1883 there *are/were* card games and guitars, not TVs.
3 There *is/was* a lot of work to do today. Can you help me?
4 There *are/were* horses and a cow for each family in a Frontier House.
5 There *are/were* lots of cars in cities now.
6 Every day *was/were* the same in 1883.

2 Change these sentences into the past simple.

1 There isn't a supermarket in our village.
   There wasn't a supermarket in our village.
2 There aren't any eggs.

3 The food isn't very good at that restaurant.

4 Cristina isn't busy.

5 Frontier houses aren't very big.

6 My mum and dad aren't happy with me.

3 Complete the blog. Use the correct form of *be* in the past simple.

My family!	⇦ ⇨
	Cancel Share Post

On Friday, my history class 1) _____*was*_____ at a museum. It 2) _____ in the town centre and there 3) _____ lots of photographs of our town in the past. In 1910 there 4) _____ many cars in the town. There 5) _____ horses and trams. The high street 6) _____ busy but the shops 7) _____ small. There 8) _____ any big supermarkets.

Support

4 Match the questions (1–6) with the answers (a–f).

1 Were your grandparents happy to see you?
2 Was the town busy on Saturday morning?
3 Was your sister at the party?
4 Were you and your brother in bed at 10 o'clock?
5 Was Daniel in class yesterday?
6 Was I good in the show?

a Yes, we were.
b Yes, they were.
c Yes, he was.
d Yes, you were.
e Yes, she was.
f Yes, it was.

5 Make negative short answers.

1 Was your uncle at the sports centre?
   No, he wasn't.
2 Were there any oranges in the cupboard?

3 Was it foggy yesterday?

4 Were you at home on Sunday, Amelia?

5 Were the chicken sandwiches OK?

6 Was your mum on the train yesterday afternoon?

6 Complete the conversation. Use the past simple of *be* and short answers.

1 **Alejandro:** _____*Were*_____ there many cafés in town?
   Granddad: No, *there weren't*.
2 **Alejandro:** _____ there a cinema?
   Granddad: Yes, _____.
3 **Alejandro:** _____ you a pilot?
   Granddad: Yes, _____.
4 **Alejandro:** _____ Mum a good student?
   Granddad: No, _____.
5 **Alejandro:** _____ Grandma a good dancer?
   Granddad: Yes, _____.
6 **Alejandro:** _____ the shops different in town?
   Granddad: Yes, _____.
7 **Alejandro:** _____ there many houses in our street?
   Granddad: No, _____.

Past simple: regular verbs

7 **Make the past simple form of these verbs.**

1	talk	*talked*	**5**	change
2	stop		**6**	travel
3	arrive		**7**	walk
4	tidy			

8 **Choose the correct answer, A, B or C.**

1 The train _____*didn't*_____ arrive at 9.30.
   A wasn't   **B** isn't   **C** didn't

2 She _____ her parents after the party.
   A text   **B** texted   **C** did text

3 They _____ us to cook dinner.
   A didn't help   **B** helps   **C** not helped

4 We _____ a film last night, but it wasn't very good.
   A watched   **B** was watching   **C** watch

5 Michele _____ computer games last night.
   A wasn't playing   **B** didn't play   **C** play

6 We _____ the kitchen before my parents arrived.
   A cleaning   **B** clean   **C** cleaned

9 **Complete the sentences about last Sunday. Use the past simple in the positive or negative form.**

	visit his/her grandparents	tidy his/her room	play volleyball
David	✓	✗	✗
Nerea	✗	✓	✓
Alba	✓	✗	✓

1 David ____*visited*____ his grandparents.
2 Nerea _____ her grandparents.
3 Nerea and Alba _____ volleyball.
4 David _____ volleyball.
5 David and Alba _____ their rooms.
6 Nerea _____ her room.

10 **Correct the sentences. Use the past simple in the positive or negative form.**

1 John Lennon played the drums.
    John Lennon didn't play the drums.
2 Christopher Columbus arrived in America in 1942.
    _____
3 Julius Caesar travelled by bus.
    _____
4 Michelangelo didn't visit Rome.
    _____
5 In 1750 people cleaned their teeth every day.
    _____
6 In 1920 most people didn't walk to school.
    _____

11 **Complete the article with these verbs. Use the past simple in the positive or negative form.**

> ~~arrive~~   change   help   play   talk
> travel   wash   watch

Pop star!

Mason playing live

A pop star – but not to his mum and dad!
Mason is a famous pop star, but he lives with his parents. He 1) ___*arrived*___ home from a concert yesterday evening. He travelled by train .He 2) _____ by helicopter, because he doesn't like flying. He always changes after a concert, so he 3) _____ his clothes and he 4) _____ his hair. He 5) _____ TV – there aren't any TVs in his parents' house. Mason 6) _____ to his parents about the concert. They talked about other things. He likes to cook, so he 7) _____ his parents to make dinner. He 8) _____ his guitar because he doesn't like to play it after a concert.

Young people, big ideas!

VOCABULARY

1 Match the pictures with these verbs, then write the past simple forms.

~~buy~~   give   sing   study   win   write

1

buy
bought

2
....
....

3

....
....

4
....
....

5

....
....

6

....
....

2 Complete the table.

Infinitive	Past simple form
1) ....*find*........	found
2)	went
3)	learned
4)	left
5)	said
6)	saw

3 Match the verbs (1–6) with the past simple forms (a–f).

1 become   a turned
2 have   b made
3 make   c became
4 start   d wanted
5 turn   e had
6 want   f started

4 Choose the correct answer, A, B or C.

1 Lilka _gave_ me a picture for my birthday. She made it for me.
  A had   B saw   **C** gave

2 I _____ to play the guitar when I was seven.
  A turned   B started   C found

3 We _____ the film at the cinema last Saturday.
  A saw   B made   C won

4 My mum is a good cook. She _____ a fantastic chicken salad for me yesterday.
  A wrote   B made   C became

5 The train for London _____ at 10.30.
  A left   B bought   C learned

6 The boys _____ the football match 5–1.
  A studied   B wanted   C won

7 London is amazing! My cousins _____ there last July.
  A said   B went   C wanted

5 Complete the sentences with the verbs in brackets. Use the past simple form.

1 I _____bought_____ (buy) a guitar last week. I'm learning to play.

2 Jessica _____ (study) a lot before the exam.

3 Charles Dickens _____ (write) the book *Oliver Twist* in 1838.

4 The children were very good, they _____ (play) together all afternoon.

5 'I'm having fun!' she _____ (say).

6 I wasn't at school yesterday because I _____ (have) a temperature.

6 Read the clues. Rearrange the letters to make adjectives.

1 My favourite subject is English. My teacher is _____ *good* _____. dgoo

2 I liked the film but it was really _____. ads

3 Sam is _____. He can help you clean that window. lalt

4 My dogs are _____ when I arrive home. pyahp

5 Meerkats stand on their legs to look around because they are _____. tohrs

6 It's _____ to find things in this room. Tidy it! fiflcudi

7 Choose the correct words.

1 My brother plays the drums. They're very *loud*/long.

2 Stefan's got a new motorbike . He's *happy/easy*.

3 You can study in the living room. It's *slow/quiet* there.

4 Rita is a *clean/good* actor. She works in the theatre.

5 The talent show is for adults. Liam is a *young/short* boy, so he can't sing in it.

6 I've got a *bad/tall* cough.

7 Andrea says maths is *fast/easy*, but I don't like it.

8 Make sentences about the photos. Use these words and the verb *be*.

difficult   dirty   fast   happy   ~~old~~   tall

1

It's old.

2

3

4

5

6

_____   _____

9 Read the conversation and choose the best answer, A, B or C.

Justine: Is this you in the photo? You look quite 1) *young* .

Mum: Yes, I was about 12. Oh! That was a 2) _____ day.

Justine: Was it a new bike?

Mum: Yes. My parents bought it for my birthday. It wasn't 3) _____ to ride.

Justine: It looks 4) _____.

Mum: Yes, it wasn't a very fast bike. But I loved it. It was usually 5) _____ because I cycled all around the village.

Justine: Who is that 6) _____ boy next to you?

Mum: That's your Uncle Val.

Justine: Really? He's 7) _____ in this photo.

Mum: I know. He wanted a bike, too!

1 A short   (B) young   C sad
2 A easy   B short   C happy
3 A sad   B easy   C loud
4 A slow   B happy   C clean
5 A short   B dirty   C difficult
6 A fast   B loud   C tall
7 A sad   B quiet   C bad

10 Read and solve the puzzle. Write the names of the horses.

1 _____ *Bella* _____   **Lightning**
2 _____   **Ned**
3 _____   **Bella**
4 _____   **Ruby**
5 _____   **Jet**
6 _____   **Buddy**

Lightning is a fast horse. He is between the tall horse and the bad horse. Ruby is next to the old horse. The bad horse isn't Jet. Buddy isn't tall or loud. Bella is the old horse. Jet is next to Ruby. Ned is next to the bad horse. He's loud.

GRAMMAR
Past simple: irregular verbs

1 **Rewrite the sentences in the past simple.**

1 1922: Howard Carter finds Tutankhamun's tomb in Egypt.

Howard Carter found Tutankhamun's tomb in Egypt in 1922.

2 1969: Neil Armstrong goes to the moon.

3 1957: Elvis Presley sings *Jailhouse Rock* for the first time.

4 2010: Spain win the football World Cup.

5 Around 1590: William Shakespeare writes *Romeo and Juliet*.

6 2009: Barack Obama becomes president of the USA.

7 2008: Catherine Hardwicke makes the first *Twilight* film.

2 **Complete the article with the verbs in brackets in the negative past simple.**

This week in **Running Wild**, Paula Clifford tells us about a running race she did across the Sahara Desert in Africa with a group of other runners.
"It was a great trip but it 1) ___*wasn't*___ (be) always fun. I was with the same ten people every day and I 2) _____ (have) any time alone - sometimes we were all very tired and we 3) _____ (want) to talk. We 4) _____ (eat) any fresh food for a month, just pasta and rice, and I 5) _____ (sleep) well in the tent. I 6) _____ (know) it was cold in the desert at night and I 7) _____ (have) warm clothes – I was always freezing! But the experience was amazing and we all became friends. I 8) _____ (win) the race across the desert but I learned a lot about myself."

3 **Read the answers. Complete the questions.**

1 **A:** ___*Did*___ you ___*see*___ Mum?
  B: Yes, I did. I saw her at the supermarket.

2 **A:** _____ you _____ the tickets?
  B: No, we didn't. You have to buy them tomorrow.

3 **A:** _____ he _____ Helen the bag?
  B: Yes, he did. He gave her the mobile phone, too.

4 **A:** _____ they _____ after lunch?
  B: Yes, they did. They left at half past two.

5 **A:** _____ she _____ dinner at home?
  B: Yes, she did. She had dinner with her family.

6 **A:** _____ you _____ a lot?
  B: Yes, I did. I wrote ten pages.

4 **Make questions. Use these verbs in the past simple and start with *Did*.**

arrive   play   start   ~~travel~~   walk   want

1 Yuri Gagarin / in space
  Did Yuri Gagarin travel in space?

2 Ed Stafford / along the Amazon River

3 John Lennon / the drums

4 Alejandro Sanz / playing the guitar when he was a boy

5 Kristen Stewart / to be famous

6 Maria Sharapova / in the USA when she was six

5 **Choose the correct answer, A, B or C.**

1 Did you leave your book at school?
  A Yes, I do.   **B** Yes, I did.
  C Yes, it did.

2 Did Clare turn off the TV?
  A No, she wasn't.   **B** No, she didn't.
  C No, she hasn't.

3 Did Chelsea win the football match?
  A Yes, we did.   **B** Yes, she did.
  C Yes, they did.

4 Did they like the salad?
  A Yes, they did.   **B** Yes, you did.
  C Yes, they were.

Past simple: wh-questions

6 **Choose the correct words.**

1 *What/Where* did you go on holiday?
2 When *was/did* you finish your homework?
3 What *did/was* the teacher say?
4 *Was/Did* the music loud?
5 *When/What* did the film start?
6 Where *did/was* the party?
7 *Why/Who* didn't you buy the motorbike?

7 **Choose the correct answer, A, B or C.**

1 _____ *When* _____ did the bus arrive?
   (**A**) When   **B** Where   **C** How
2 _____ won the competition?
   A What   **B** Why   **C** Who
3 _____ film did you see?
   A Where   **B** What   **C** When
4 _____ didn't you say 'hello'?
   A Why   **B** What   **C** Who
5 _____ did you go on holiday?
   A Where   **B** What   **C** How
6 _____ was the food?
   A When   **B** Why   **C** How

8 **Put the words in the correct order to make questions.**

1 that / she / message? / did / write / Why
   Why did she write that message?
2 favourite / was / picture? / What / your
3 the / train /did / leave? / When
4 did / sister / your / to / go / school? / Where
5 did / Who / see / you / the / café? / at
6 Where / find / the / book? / did / geography / you

9 **Match the questions (1–7) with the answers (a–g).**

1 Where did you go with your school?
2 What did you see?
3 Who did you go with?
4 How did you find all the places?
5 What did you have for lunch?
6 Why did you go?
7 When did you arrive home?

a To practise our English.
b We went to London.
c We had a map.
d Ten students from my class.
e We had lots of sandwiches.
f Last Saturday.
g We saw museums and famous places.

10 **Make questions about Steven Spielberg. Use these verbs.**

be   ~~be born~~   become   learn   make
start   study   win

Steven Spielberg

Name: Steven Spielberg

1 Born: 1946, Cincinnati, USA
2 Studied at California State University
3 Became a film-maker in 1969
4 Learned to be a film-maker at Universal Studios
5 First films: adventure films
6 Made *Jaws* in 1975
7 Won the Academy Award for *Schindler's List* in 1993
8 Started making films because he wanted to tell adventure stories

1 (Where) _____ *Where was he born?*
2 (Where) _____
3 (When) _____
4 (Where) _____
5 (What) _____
6 (When) _____
7 (When) _____
8 (Why) _____

Revision Units 7 – 8

VOCABULARY

1 Rearrange the letters to make ordinal numbers.
Then put the cardinal numbers.

1 rihrtd _____third_____ _____3_____
2 tsifr _____ _____
3 ighhet _____ _____
4 thewflt _____ _____
5 txeeishtn _____ _____
6 iewenttht _____ _____
7 ytewnt-cendos _____ _____

2 Match the dates (1–6) with the way we write them (a–f).

1 the fifth of March nineteen ten
2 the fifteenth of March nineteen ninety
3 the fifth of May nineteen nineteen
4 the fifteenth of May nineteen ten
5 the fifth of March nineteen oh nine
6 the fifth of March nineteen ninety-nine

a 5 March 1999
b 5 March 1909
c 15 May 1910
d 5 March 1910
e 5 May 1919
f 15 March 1990

3 Complete the table with these verbs.

> arrive at   ~~buy~~   give   go to   play   sing
> stay at   write

1) _____buy_____ ... a present
2) _____
3) _____ ... a friend's house
4) _____
5) _____
6) _____ ... a song
7) _____
8) _____

4 Choose the correct answer, A, B or C.

1 My friend _made_ us some pasta yesterday evening.
   A saw   (B) made   C cleaned
2 Did you _____ your room at the weekend?
   A tidy   B travel   C arrive
3 I can't _____ my mobile phone! Where is it?
   A talk   B turn   C find
4 We _____ to the cinema last night. The film was really good.
   A won   B went   C wrote
5 Steven Spielberg _____ a film-maker when he was just 23.
   A arrived   B became   C went

5 Find and make the opposites of these adjectives.

difficult _____easy_____   loud _____
short _____   slow _____
old _____   happy _____
dirty _____

q	t	s	c	l	q	f	a	s	t
u	a	y	o	n	t	u	m	f	e
c	l	n	e	a	s	y	i	c	b
c	l	f	s	s	a	o	e	e	o
s	w	e	a	t	d	u	s	u	t
p	q	u	a	p	t	n	t	q	r
a	y	u	o	n	s	g	b	z	x

6 Complete the text. Use the opposites of the words in brackets.

Excelsior Hotel

Excelsior Hotel   **Overall rating: ★★**

This hotel is 1) (difficult) _____easy_____ to find. It's next to the bus station. Our room was 2) (clean) _____ and we didn't sleep because it was very 3) (quiet) _____ outside. There were 4) (not many) _____ buses.
We visited in November and the hotel was 5) (hot) _____.
The room service was 6) (fast) _____, too.
We didn't have a 7) (bad) _____ holiday at the Excelsior.

GRAMMAR

1 Complete the sentences with *is*, *are*, *was* or *were*.

1 The train _____*was*_____ fast but quiet.
2 There _____ 25 people at the party yesterday.
3 Look! _____ that your brother over there?
4 The teacher _____ (not) very happy with me on Monday. I didn't do my homework.
5 It _____ (not) easy to clean a house in the past.
6 How many stairs _____ there in your house?
7 _____ you at the sports centre yesterday afternoon?

2 Complete the paragraph with these verbs. Use the past simple form.

> arrive   be   buy   go   not stay   study
> travel   win

My grandfather 1) _____*was*_____ very young when he 2) _____ in the USA. His parents 3) _____ there from Italy to work. He 4) _____ science and he 5) _____ a prize. He 6) _____ in the USA. He 7) _____ to a lot of different countries and 8) _____ a house in Australia. Now he lives in Sydney. We usually visit him in the summer.

3 Choose the correct answer, A, B or C.

1 Did you find your bag?
  (A) Yes, I did.   **B** Yes, I do.
  C Yes, it did.
2 Was it your birthday on the fourth?
  A Yes, it is.   **B** Yes, it was.
  C Yes, I am.
3 Did your parents help you do your homework?
  A No, they don't.   **B** No, they didn't.
  C No, they weren't.
4 Did I really say that?
  A Yes, you were.   **B** Yes, you are.
  C Yes, you did.
5 Were the trams slow today?
  A Yes, they were.   **B** Yes, it was.
  C Yes, there were.
6 Were there any crisps on the table?
  A Yes, they did.   **B** Yes, they were.
  C Yes, there were.

4 Choose the correct words.

Interviewer: Hello, Donald. Thank you for talking to me today.
Donald: That's OK. Please call me Don.
Interviewer: My first question is why did you 1) *become/became* a singer?
Donald: Because I 2) *love/loved* singing when I was a boy.
Interviewer: And where did you 3) *learned/learn* to sing?
Donald: I didn't 4) *have/had* singing lessons. I learned from my dad.
Interviewer: When 5) *did/have* you make your first CD? Was it in 1984?
Donald: Yes. When I was 18. When I 6) *did leave/left* school.
Interviewer: Really? And did you 7) *play/played* the guitar at school?
Donald: No, I 8) *didn't/don't*. I started to play in 1988, after my second CD.

5 Read the answers and make *wh-* questions. Use the past simple.

1 Q When _____*did you visit Warsaw?*_____
  A I visited Warsaw last spring.
2 Q When _____?
  A The party was on Saturday evening.
3 Q What _____?
  A We talked about computer games.
4 Q Why _____?
  A She became a photographer because she loved taking photos.
5 Q Where _____?
  A The group's first show was in Granada.
6 Q Why _____?
  A My little sister was happy because she went to a party.
7 Q How _____?
  A They travelled to the forest by bike.

09 Head to toe

VOCABULARY

1 Match the pictures with these words and phrases.

curly   long fair   ~~long wavy~~
short and straight   spiky   wavy

1

2

long wavy

3

4

5

6

2 Rearrange the letters to make hairstyles.

1 yavw   *wavy*
2 nolg   ....
3 lrcuy   ....
4 ksiyp   ....
5 sorht   ....
6 gtsiarht   ....

3 Put the words in the correct order.

1 got / dark / hair. / I've / curly
      I've got curly dark hair.
2 Owen's / spiky / hair. / got / short
   ....
3 long / hair. / like / I / straight
   ....
4 wants / curly / She / hair. / long
   ....
5 boy's / fair / wavy / That / got / hair.
   ....
6 got / long / red / sister's / My / hair.
   ....

4 Look and make sentences about the hairstyles. Use *have got*.

1

2

She's got long curly hair.

3

4

5

6

5 Find eight parts of the body.

e	y	b	a	c	k	m	e
f	m	f	e	r	o	e	t
c	o	r	a	p	m	e	o
r	u	o	f	c	u	t	e
m	t	y	t	e	e	e	a
s	h	o	u	l	d	e	r
i	f	a	c	i	e	t	k
e	i	n	g	a	c	h	l

1 _back_   5 ....
2 ....   6 ....
3 ....   7 ....
4 ....   8 ....

6 Match the photo with these words and phrases.

fingers   knee   left hand   leg   neck
nose   ~~right hand~~

1 _right hand_	**2**

3	**4**

5	**6**

7

7 How many have you got? Complete the table with parts of the body. Use plurals if necessary.

one	two	ten
nose	knees	fingers
mouth	legs	7) ....
1) _neck_	arms	
2)	4)	
3)	5)	
	6)	

8 Choose the correct answer, A, B or C.

1 Ouch! My _finger_ is in the door!
   A back   **B** tooth   **C** finger

2 Use your .... to help you jump.
   A shoulders   **B** knees   **C** face

3 My cousin's got a bad .... She can't play volleyball today.
   A hand   **B** mouth   **C** nose

4 How is your .... ? Can you sleep OK?
   A legs   **B** back   **C** shoulders

5 I texted a lot yesterday. My .... are tired!
   A feet   **B** legs   **C** fingers

6 My uncle's a pilot. His .... are very good.
   A eyes   **B** legs   **C** shoulders

7 Atishoo! Sorry, it's my .... again! I've got a cold.
   A tooth   **B** nose   **C** face

GRAMMAR
Comparative adjectives

1 Choose the correct words.

1 The bus is usually _slower_/slow than the train.
2 English is easy/easier than Chinese.
3 Oranges are good/better for you than crisps.
4 Our computer is old/older than that one.
5 The supermarket is nearer than/that the market.
6 Pasta is nice/nicer than rice.
7 My new mobile phone is smaller/small than yours.
8 Today is sunnier then/than yesterday.

2 Read and choose the best answer, A, B or C.

Subject: **My new house!**

Hi Nathalie,
How are you? Is your arm 1) _better_ now?
We've got a new house. It's 2) _____ than
the old house. It's 3) _____ to find, too,
because it's next to the park. There aren't a lot of
cars here, so it's 4) _____ and the house is
5) _____ , too.
This house has got a big garden. Monique loves
playing in it. She's 6) _____ than she was in
the old house. She's four years old now, and she
is 7) _____ than before! It's difficult to do
my homework these days.
See you soon,
Dianne

1	**A** best	**B** bigger	**C** better
2	**A** bigger	**B** big	**C** biggest
3	**A** easier	**B** easiest	**C** worse
4	**A** louder	**B** quieter	**C** older
5	**A** curlier	**B** cleanest	**C** cleaner
6	**A** sadder	**B** happy	**C** happier
7	**A** loud	**B** louder	**C** quieter

3 Complete the text with these adjectives in the comparative form.

curly   good   happy   loud   short   tall   ~~young~~

My family
by Wiktor Jeziorska

Here's a photo of some of the people in my
family. You can see my mum and dad behind
me, and also my uncle Borys. He's dad's 1)
younger brother, but he's 2) _____
than him. I've got two sisters. They're twins.
They look the same, but Anastasia's hair is
3) _____ than Ala's.
My cousin Dobry is 11. His hair is short like
mine, but it's 4) _____ than my hair.
Marek is Dobry's little brother. In this photo,
Dobry is 5) _____ than Marek, but usually
Marek is happy and much 6) _____ than
his brother. We play computer games together
and Marek wins because he is 7) _____
than me.

4 Make sentences. Use the adjectives in the comparative form.

1 my grandfather / my grandmother (old)
My grandfather is older than my grandmother.
2 planes / trains (fast)
_____
3 the kitchen / the living room (dirty)
_____
4 your singing / my singing (bad)
_____
5 art / maths (easy)
_____
6 pandas / meerkats (big)
_____

Superlative adjectives

5 Complete the table.

adjective	superlative
easy	the easiest
1) _____ *slow*	the slowest
big	2) _____
funny	3) _____
4) _____	the worst
sad	5) _____
good	6) _____
nice	7) _____

6 Rewrite the sentences. Use the opposites in the superlative form.

1 My brother's bedroom is <u>the cleanest</u> in the house.
   My brother's bedroom is the dirtiest in the house.

2 I think this is <u>the best</u> DVD I've got.

3 I've got three cousins. Rafael is <u>the shortest</u>.

4 This is <u>the saddest</u> day of my life.

5 Our classroom is <u>the hottest</u> in the school.

6 They've got three dogs. Pablo is <u>the quietest</u>.

7 Complete the sentences with these adjectives in the superlative form.

~~bad~~   fast   good   long   small   young

1 Eddie Edwards was the _____ *worst* _____ ski jumper in the world. But he was the best in Britain!

2 The AVE Talgo 350 in Spain is one of the _____ trains in Europe. It travels at 330 kilometres an hour.

3 The _____ house in Britain is in Conwy, Wales. There are only two rooms – one upstairs and one downstairs.

4 Praia do Cassino in Brazil is the world's _____ beach. It's about 240 kilometres long.

5 The _____ driver to win the Formula 1 championship was Sebastian Vettel. He was 23 years old.

6 I think Robert De Niro is the _____ actor in the world. I love all his films.

8 Complete the website with these adjectives in the superlative form.

bad   ~~cold~~   hot   nice   rainy   snowy

Moscow, Russia's beautiful capital city

Q: What's the weather like in Moscow?

A: The 1) _____ *coldest* _____ months in Moscow are January and February. The temperature is usually around -9°C. The first snow is in October and it stays until April. February 2010 was the 2) _____ month in Moscow for 40 years, with 425,000 m³ of snow.

   In summer the temperature is usually about 18°C. The 3) _____ months are July and August, when the temperature can be 30°C during the day.

   The 4) _____ months are July and August, with around 90mm of rain.

Q When is the best time to visit Moscow?

A: This is a difficult question. There is something to see in every season. Maybe the 5) _____ time to visit is the beginning of spring or end of autumn, because the weather is very cloudy, cold and rainy. The 6) _____ time is in the summer or the winter.

VOCABULARY

1 Complete the table with these words.

> camping   rock climbing   rollerblading
> shopping   skateboarding   surfing
> ~~swimming~~

sea	countryside	town
1) _swimming_	3)	5)
2)	4)	6)
		7)

2 Rearrange the letters to make sports or fun activities.

1   nisnet   _tennis_
2   aaelblbs
3   gknsii
4   cnaidgn
5   lgyccin
6   ktslbbaela
7   ceahb bvlloeylal

3 Complete the speech bubbles with *play* or *go*.

On holiday

We asked some teenagers about their favourite holiday activities. This is what they said ...

1 We usually ___go___ skiing in the mountains in France. I love skiing!

2 I often _____ tennis with my dad when we are on holiday.

3 We _____ camping next to the lake every summer. It's fantastic!

4 My sisters _____ shopping every day on holiday. But I don't like it.

5 I love to _____ beach volleyball. It's my favourite sport!

6 My family don't like staying on the beach. We _____ surfing or swimming.

4 Rerite the sentences in the past simple.

1   I go dancing on Sunday.
_____ _I went dancing on Sunday._
2   She plays tennis at the sports centre.
_____
3   Do you play baseball on Friday?
_____
4   They go skiing in January.
_____
5   Do you go camping near the sea?
_____
6   Does he play basketball at school?
_____
7   My dog goes swimming in the river.
_____

5 Read and choose the best answer, A, B or C.

Free time!   ⇦ ⇨

Cancel   Share   Post

In my free time I love to go 1) _dancing_ with my friends. We have lots of fun! I don't go 2) _____ with my sister. She says it's great, but I think it's difficult. We play 3) _____ together and I usually win!
I go 4) _____ at the weekends in the countryside or in the park. It's very good for me and I have a great bike. At school we play 5) _____ every Tuesday. I don't play 6) _____. My brother plays it with his class. He says it's fun!

Support

1   **A** basketball   **B** tennis   **C** dancing
2   **A** beach volleyball   **B** rollerblading   **C** baseball
3   **A** surfing   **B** hopping   **C** tennis
4   **A** cycling   **B** camping   **C** swimming
5   **A** skateboarding   **B** skiing   **C** basketball
6   **A** dancing   **B** baseball   **C** rock climbing

6 Look at the pictures. Complete the crossword puzzle.

| 1 | 2 | 3 | 4 across |
| 4 down | 5 | 6 | 7 |

	¹J	A	C	K	E	²T		³	

7 Write the words you can use with 'a pair of'. Use the plural form. You do not need all the words.

~~boot~~ hat jacket
jeans sandal
shirt shoe shorts
skirt sunglasses
sweatshirt
swimsuit tights
trainer T-shirt

A pair of…
boots
....
....
....
....
....
....

8 Choose the correct words.

1 It's sunny. I need my *sunglasses*/tights.
2 It's windy. I'm wearing my *shorts/jacket*.
3 It's rainy. I've got my *boots/sandals* on.
4 It's cool. Wear your *shorts/jeans*.
5 It's hot. Where are my *boots/shorts*?
6 It's wet. Put on a *hat/T-shirt*.

9 Complete the sentences.

1

I'm going to buy some b _o o t s_ and a h _a t_ .

2

I've got my sw _____ and a pair of sun _____ .

3
I'm going to wear a sh _____ and a j _____ .

4

I'm going to stay at home in my je _____ and sw _____ .

5

I'm going to play tennis in my sh _____ and a T- _____ .

10 Complete the blog with these words.

boots sandals ~~shirts~~ shorts
sunglasses swimsuits

" On Saturdays I help in my parents' clothes shop. There are a lot of different clothes in our shop. There are 1) ___*shirts*___ and jackets for special parties or sports clothes, for example 2) _____ for the pool. Our 3) _____ and T-shirts are good for going to the beach on holiday. I like the 4) _____ we've got. They are fantastic for your eyes on very sunny days. We've got shoes for different weather: 5) _____ in the summer and 6) _____ in the winter. "

GRAMMAR
Going to

1 Look at the photos. Make sentences with *going to*.

1 .... *They're going to go rollerblading.* ....
2 ....
3 ....
4 ....
5 ....
6 ....

2 Rewrite the sentences in the negative form.

1 We're going to win.
   .... *We aren't going to win.* ....
2 He's going to sing in the show.
   ....
3 They're going to have a party.
   ....
4 I'm going to go shopping.
   ....
5 You're going to clean your bedroom.
   ....
6 She's going to go dancing.
   ....

3 Complete the conversation with *be going to* in the correct form.

Dave: Where are you going?
Rob: To the shops in the town centre.
Dave: What 1) ___*are*___ you *going to* buy?
Rob: Some new clothes for my holiday in Australia. We 2) _____ visit my aunt and uncle.
Dave: Wow! What kind of clothes do you want?
Rob: Well … My aunt and uncle live near the sea, so I 3) _____ buy a swimsuit.
Dave: Good idea. 4) _____ you _____ get some sunglasses, too?
Rob: Yes, I am. And some shorts and T-shirts, because it 5) _____ be sunny and hot.
Dave: Hmm. 6) _____ n't it _____ be difficult to find shorts and T-shirts in the shops? It's December!

4 Make positive (+) or negative (–) short answers.

1 Are you going to go surfing this summer? (–)
   .... *No, I'm not.* ....
2 Is he going to go dancing with his friends? (+)
   ....
3 Are we going to go swimming this afternoon? (+)
   ....
4 Are they going to go cycling tomorrow? (–)
   ....
5 Am I going to play basketball for the school? (+)
   ....
6 Is it going to rain at the football match? (–)
   ....

5 Make questions. Use *going to* in the correct form.

1 you / go to Disneyland in the summer
   Are you going to go to Disneyland in the summer?
2 you / travel by plane
   ....
3 the weather / be hot
   ....
4 your sister / go with you
   ....
5 you all / stay in a hotel
   ....
6 the holiday / be in the summer
   ....

Want + to + infinitive, Like/Love + -ing

6 **Choose the correct words.**

1 What do you want *doing/to do* on holiday?
2 We love *play/playing* tennis in the summer.
3 Francesco and Sergio want *to go/going* shopping.
4 My brother likes *playing/play* basketball.
5 I want *to go/going* camping.
6 What does Beata like *do/doing* at the weekends?

7 **Complete the sentences with the correct form of these verbs, in the infinitive or –ing form.**

~~be~~   go   listen   play   stay   tidy   watch

1 My cousin wants ___*to be*___ a dancer.
2 I don't like _____ my bedroom.
3 Does your friend want _____ to some music with us?
4 My sister loves _____ TV in the afternoon.
5 I don't like _____ dancing with my parents.
6 Do you want _____ at home in the holidays?
7 The students love _____ computer games at lunchtime.

8 **Choose the correct answer, A, B or C.**

1 What time do you want ___*to go*___ shopping?
   A going   **(B)** to go   C to want
2 Stella loves _____ skiing.
   A to play   B playing   C going
3 We want _____ English every day!
   A to study   B learning   C studying
4 My parents like _____ to France on holiday.
   A to go   B travelling   C to travel
5 Do you want _____ a basketball player?
   A learning   B to learn   C to be
6 I love _____ my friends after school.
   A to study   B to meet   C meeting

9 **Put the conversation in the correct order.**

Maria: But you love playing sport. You can study sports science at university. _____
Maria: Yes, I do. I want to be a doctor. I like studying science. _____
Kara: No, I don't … but I don't want to go to university. I don't like studying! _____
Kara: Yes, that's true. I like going swimming and playing football. What about you? You don't like playing sports. Do you know what you want to be? _____
Kara: A doctor? That's fantastic. _____
Maria: Do you know what you want to study after school? __*1*__

10 **Read the notes and the text about James. Complete the text about Alex with verbs in the infinitive or -ing form.**

View previous comments   Cancel   Share   Post

Name: James
Home town: Cambridge
Age: 14
Likes: computer games, guitar lessons
Dislikes: shopping, skiing
Favourite subject: science
Favourite job: pilot
Dream: visit Africa

View previous comments   Cancel   Share   Post

Name: Alex
Home town: Manchester
Age: 15
Likes: tennis, travel
Dislikes: TV, swimming
Favourite subject: art
Favourite job: photographer
Dream: write a book

James likes playing computer games. He likes having guitar lessons. He doesn't like going shopping or going skiing. His favourite subject is science. He wants to be a pilot and he wants to visit Africa.

Alex likes 1) ___*playing*___ tennis and he likes 2) _____ . He doesn't like 3) _____ TV or 4) _____ swimming. His favourite subject is art. He wants 5) _____ a photographer and he wants 6) _____ a book one day.

Revision Units 9 – 10

VOCABULARY

1 Complete the sentences.

1 I've got a problem with my left s _houlder_ .
2 She's got long, w_____ hair.
3 Wash your h_____ before you have lunch.
4 Yuri's hair isn't the same as his brother's. It's
   f_____, not dark.
5 Is your little f_____r OK now?
6 Dad's got a bad l_____ because he played
   football yesterday.
7 My best friend's got curly hair, but she wants
   s_____t hair.

2 Label the picture with these clothes words.

> boot   jacket   ~~jeans~~   sandal   shirt
> shorts   skirt   trainer

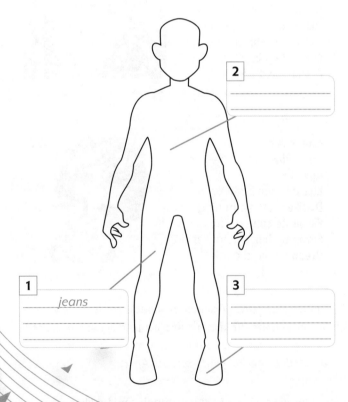

1 _jeans_
2
3

3 Match 1–7 with a–g to make clothes and sports words.

1	volley	a	blading
2	skate	b	ing
3	sun	c	suit
4	sweat	d	boarding
5	roller	e	ball
6	swim	f	glasses
7	ski	g	shirt

4 Find four fun activities and four parts of the body.

s	h	o	l	t	n	s	z	t
h	y	d	i	e	o	h	p	e
e	h	c	a	n	s	o	a	n
k	a	n	y	n	u	p	t	n
t	n	f	o	i	c	p	i	h
a	d	e	i	s	r	i	e	a
k	n	l	e	n	e	n	n	w
c	y	c	l	i	n	g	s	g

1 _tennis_   5 _____
2 _____   6 _____
3 _____   7 _____
4 _____   8 _____

5 Complete the conversation.

A: It's cold today, don't you think?
B: Yes. I need a 1) h _a t_ .
A: I'm glad I've got my 2) t_____ on with
   this skirt, but my 3) h_____ are cold.
A: Would you like to go to the beach?
B: Yes, but I haven't got my
   4) s_____t.
A: That's OK. We can wear 5) s_____s and
   6) T-_____. It's a bit windy for
   swimming, anyway.

GRAMMAR

1 Choose the correct answer, A, B or C.

1 Cycling is _faster_ than walking.
   A slower   B fast   **C** faster

2 These sunglasses are _____ than my old sunglasses.
   A nice   B nicer   C nicest

3 He didn't want _____ shopping with us on Saturday.
   A to go   B going   C go

4 Yolanda loves _____ beach volleyball on holiday.
   A play   B playing   C plays

5 Writing a text is _____ than writing an email.
   A difficult   B easiest   C easier

6 That's _____ café in the town centre.
   A bad   B worse   C the worst

7 Do you like camping or _____ in a hotel?
   A staying   B to stay   C stay

8 _Memories_ is _____ song on the CD.
   A sadder   B the saddest   C sad

2 Read about Emilie's friends. Put the correct names under the photographs.

> Anna's got the curliest hair. Heidi's hair is the longest. Isabel hasn't got the shortest hair and she hasn't got straight hair. Marta's hair is shorter than Jana's and Eva's hair. Eva's mouth is bigger than Jana's mouth.

1	2
Anna	
3	4
5	6

3 Complete the sentences. Use the correct form of _going to_ and these verbs.

> ~~be~~   fly   go   have   play   see   watch

1 My mum _'s going to be_ happy when she sees my bedroom. It's clean!

2 I _____ a shower before I go to the party.

3 It's not very near here. We _____ by car. The train is easier.

4 _____ Cristian _____ card games with us tomorrow?

5 There aren't any good programmes on tonight. I _____ TV.

6 _____ the bats _____ near us in the cave?

7 He _____ his favourite band in concert on Saturday night.

4 Make questions. Use the verbs in the correct form (infinitive or _-ing_).

1 you / like / go / to the beach
   Do you like going to the beach?

2 your dad / like / make lunch / on Sunday
   _____

3 Helena / want / learn / French
   _____

4 pandas / like / swim
   _____

5 your parents / want / go / camping this year
   _____

6 you / like / play / basketball
   _____

5 Complete the blog with one word in each space.

💬 View previous comments   Cancel   Share   Post

Hi! I'm Antonio. I live near the sea and I'm happy because I 1) _like_ swimming. I often go to the beach and I love 2) _____ my friends there. It's fun. We think it's much 3) _____ than staying at home. We don't like 4) _____ computer games or card games. They're boring! I want 5) _____ be a swimming teacher so I have to practise my swimming every day. It's 6) _____ to swim in a swimming pool, because it's warmer and there's no wind. But I love 7) _____ in the sea. I'm 8) _____ to go swimming at the beach now!

Write a comment   Support

Pearson Education Limited
Edinburgh Gate
Harlow
Essex CM20 2JE
England
and Associated Companies throughout the world.

www.pearsonelt.com

© Pearson Education Limited 2014

The right of Lucy Frino to be identified as authors of this Work has been
asserted by her in accordance with the Copyright, Designs and Patents
Act 1988.

All rights reserved; no part of this publication may be reproduced,
stored in a retrieval system, or transmitted in any form or by any means,
electronic, mechanical, photocopying, recording, or otherwise without
the prior written permission of the Publishers

First published 2014
Eighth impression 2018

ISBN: 978-1-4479-1387-0

Set in 10pt Mixage ITC Std
Print and bound in Malaysia (CTP-PJB)

The publisher would like to thank the following for their kind
permission to reproduce their photographs:

(Key: b-bottom; c-centre; l-left; r-right; t-top)

Alamy Images: Ned Bennett 49r, Beyond Fotomedia GmbH 52tr,
Clearview 24bc, Rob Cousins 8l, Cultura Creative 23c (museum
attendant), David Noton Photography 23c (park), Design Pics Inc 16bl,
Matt Ellis 26cl, Eric Gevaert 26tl, Hero Images Inc. 41cr, George H.H.
Huey 16br, Ilene MacDonald 11tl, Francisco Martinez 31tl, Maged
Michel 17tr, Keith Morris 31bl, 31br, OJO Images Ltd 11cr, Parker
Photography 46cl, Paul Mayall Australia 17tl, Prisma Bildagentur AG
11tr, Radius Images 23c (class), Mike Rex 9tl, Gary Roebuck 51c, Chris
Rout 31cl, 31cr, Alex Segre 23b, Adrian Sherratt 33t, Tom Wood 41bl;
Bahamas Tourist Office: 16cr (shark); **Bananastock:** 46tl; **Corbis:**
Tammy Hanratty 51bc, MM Productions 41cl, Ocean 37b, Albert Pena
47bl, Wavebreak Media 33bc; **Digital Vision:** 16cl (bear); **DK Images:**
34bc, Rosemary Bailey 51tr, Bonetti 20r, Gerard Brown 52cl, Terry
Carter 18b, Claire Cordier 24tc (bridge), Andy Holligan 16cr (goat),
Jamie Marshall 17cr, Ian O'Leary 34tl, Stephen Oliver 26bl, Gary
Ombler 16cl (bat), Helena Smith 7bc, James Tye 24bl; **FLPA Images
of Nature:** Minden Pictures / Rene Krekels 17br; **Fotolia.com:** Africa
Studio 34br, Jacek Chabraszewski 21t, Les Cunliffe 24tc (jungle),
Dalibor 16tl, Dezperado 26tr, Sonya Etchison 52tc, David Hughes
41tl, Joda 51tl, Michael Mill 17cl, Claudia Nagel 31tr, Photosvac
17bl, RichG 23t, rolero54 34cr, Silver-john 19l, Ferenc Szelepcsenyi
23c (cinema), Taxiberlin 26cr; **Getty Images:** Amriphoto 52tc, John
Borthwick 52br, Jon Boyes 41tr, Nancy R. Cohen 52, Image Source
12t, iStock Vectors 26br, Carey Kirkella 11cl, Kondo Photography 46br,
Steve Margala 46bl, Peter Muller 39r, Trinette Reed 7br, Sheer Photo
7tr, Taxi 4c, Tim Whitby 43r; **Imagemore Co., Ltd:** 51bl; **Imagestate
Media:** 24br; **John Foxx Images:** 41br; **Pearson Education Ltd:**
Jon Barlow 53br, MindStudio 24tl, Jules Selmes 19r, 21b, Studio 8
15b, 33b; **PhotoDisc:** 16tr, 34cl; **Photolibrary.com:** Nicole Goddard
53tr; **Shutterstock.com:** Littleny 47br; **Sozaijiten:** 24tr, 34tr, 34bl;
SuperStock: 4tl, 4tr, 7tl, 7tc, 7bl, 33tc, 46tr; **www.imagesource.com:**
46cr

Cover images: *Front:* **Corbis:** Ocean

All other images © Pearson Education

Every effort has been made to trace the copyright holders and we
apologise in advance for any unintentional omissions. We would be
pleased to insert the appropriate acknowledgement in any subsequent
edition of this publication.